Elizabeth Bookser Barkley

Loving the Everyday

MEDITATIONS FOR MOMS

St.
ANTHONY
MESSENGER
PRESS

CINCINNATI, OHIO

🐦 TO MY HUSBAND, Scott,
who from the earliest days of our life together
has reminded me to "take one day at a time."

Nihil Obstat: Hilarion Kistner, O.F.M.
　　　　　　　Rev. Robert L. Hagedorn

Imprimi Potest: John Bok, O.F.M.
　　　　　　　Provincial

Imprimatur: +Carl K. Moeddel, V.G.
　　　　　　　Archdiocese of Cincinnati
　　　　　　　October 28, 1993

The *nihil obstat* and *imprimatur* are a
declaration that a book is considered to be
free from doctrinal or moral error. It is not
implied that those who have granted the
nihil obstat and *imprimatur* agree with the
contents, opinions or statements expressed.

Cover and book design by Julie Lonneman
Cover illustrations by Paula Wiggins

ISBN 0-86716-191-4

Published by St. Anthony Messenger Press
Printed in the U.S.A.

LOVING THE EVERYDAY

CONTENTS

Introduction 1

Indications

Rocking Chair 5
So Much Noise 7
Timely Matters 9
'...And to Dust You Shall
    Return' 10
Food Blues 12
Mail Call 14
Pondering the Depths 16
Hard Work 17
Lost Weekends 19
Sibling Harmony 21

Expectations

A New Day Dawns 23
Living Day by Day 25
Parenting Goals 27
Waiting for the Light 29
Saying 'No' 31
Helping Out 33
Preserving the Temple 34
Teary-eyed 36
Winding Down 38

Progressions

The Creative Word 41
Celebrating the 'Firsts' of
    Life 43
Picturebook Memories 44

In Fear and Trembling 47
A New School Year 49
Clothed in Memories 50
The Task of Learning 53
Guileless 55
Letter to Camp 57
Good-bye, Thumb 59
Growing Up 61
Leaving Their Mark 63
Adolescence 65
Creative Resume
    Writing 67

Confrontations

Maternal Strife 69
Mean Mom 71
Blowup 73
Death of the Innocents 75
Abused 77
Power Play 79
Nag, Nag, Nag 81
Sibling Battles 83
Stinging Words 85

Affirmations

The 'Sacrament' of
    Touch 87
I'm Proud of You 89
Cries in the Night 91
Treasures Lost...and
    Found 93

Telephone Ties 95

Thank-You's 97

Workers' Compensation 99

The Joy of Pets 101

Getting to Know You 103

Old Friends 105

Vive la Difference! 107

Looking Like a Mom 109

Elder-love 111

Missing You 113

So Beautiful 115

Inspirations

Faith of Our Mothers 117

Role Model 119

Fallen Heroes 121

Teachers' Legacies 123

Transported by Books 125

'Disabled' Children 127

The Gift of Teachers 129

Quiet Time 131

The Wisdom of Age 133

Frustrations

Send in the Sun 135

At Their Own Speed 137

Over-scheduled 139

Waiting Rooms 141

Guardian Angels 143

Sick Leave 145

The Death of a Pet 147

Absentee Mom 149

Money Woes 151

Sleepless Nights 153

Accepting Defeat 155

Chronically Ill 157

Unspeakable Loss 159

Give Me Space 161

Divorce 163

Going It Alone 165

Road Trip Blues 166

Celebrations

A Joyful Noise 169

Godchild 171

High-Energy Zone 173

Peals of Laughter 175

Liturgy the Joyful Way 177

Family Gatherings 179

Savoring That Perfect
  Evening 181

Life's Bounty 182

Birthday Joys 184

Easter Visions 186

Reborn in Spring 188

Mother's Day 190

Father's Day: To My
  Husband 193

Autumn Arrives 195

The Warmth of Fire 197

Thanksgiving Day 198

Holiday Horrors 200

A New Year 202

Acknowledgments 204

Introduction

RECENTLY, WHILE PAGING through a dictionary of the Bible, I happened upon an entry entitled "mother." It listed only six references to mothers and took up less than half an inch of the dictionary page. By contrast, "Moses" covered over four pages, probably a good indication that the writers of the Bible weren't women...or mothers.

Any Christian mother takes seriously her role in helping shape the faith life of her children. Unlike Moses, she will not be handed tablets of stone to guide her in forming their character; each day will be a new challenge in interpreting the gray areas of life and morality. But in her role as mother she may feel a kinship with Moses, troubled as she is by her share of plagues on her way to the Promised Land. Moses had a chronicler of his journeys; who will record a mother's?

There seems to be a conspiracy of silence about the everyday details and emotions of mothering. After all, who would want to read about anything so routine? Partway through this book, I foundered, wondering the same thing. Then one night I listened to a gifted poet, a mother, read poems rooted in family life; her poetic stories so moved me that I renewed my commitment to sharing my journey.

Sharing is what this book is about. It's a sharing rooted in one important assumption: For a Christian, belief in God and the teachings of Jesus are supports for the vocation of parenthood. These meditations will be of little value to anyone who does not share this assumption. Because this book flows from my own experience of mothering, it bears the distinct marks of my own family: I am happily married, the daughter of supportive parents, a sibling to five sisters (some married and some not), the parent of three daughters and a woman fulfilled in a career outside the home. But as I wrote, I tried to keep in mind all those mothers who differ from me: those in abusive or nonsupportive marriages, those who are single parents, those who are mothers of boys, those who choose not to work outside the home or who go off to jobs that are more drudgery than enrichment.

The eight sections of this book sort the meditations by their tone: Some are upbeat, some are inspirational, some reflect days when I was overwhelmed by the massive task of parenting. You may want to read meditations to match what's happening on a given day in your life or you may want to turn to the section of meditations that fits your mood for the day. I suggest reading this book in snatches (what mother has time for more?). Reflect on our common experiences and consider the activity at the end of each reflection as an action or a prayer for that day.

Where to keep the book so it will be most useful? If it weren't a book for mothers, I'd suggest a night table near the bed, but I know few mothers who actually read before falling to sleep. Why not an office desk drawer, a briefcase, or even the magazine rack in the bathroom where you might find a few quiet moments for reflection?

Special thanks to St. Anthony Messenger Press for inviting me to blend my love of mothering and my love of writing in this endeavor. Special thanks also to my early readers who gave me honest feedback from the perspective of real mothers: my sisters, Cathy Bookser Feister and Barb Fraze, and my friend, Susan Porter Plageman.

Rocking Chair

Comfort, O comfort my people, says your God.
—Isaiah 40:1

W E'LL NEED A ROCKING CHAIR, I think to myself
in the early months of pregnancy. A crib, a
fresh coat of paint for the room, a throw rug
for the hardwood floor, a changing table and, of course, a
rocking chair. Every family needs a rocking chair, and
we're about to be a real family.

An enduring image from my own childhood is the
slatted wooden high-backed rocker in which I was rocked
and soothed during a bout with chicken pox. I'm not sure
I actually remember being rocked, but family legend has
it that my mother stayed up all night with me so I
wouldn't scratch the chicken pox and forever bear the
scars. My memories are as good as the reality.

That rocking chair, covered with coats of paint,
became something of a family heirloom, always a fixture
in my parents' bedroom, empty during the day when
Mother had five or six children to care for. At nights,

though, in the half-awake hours, I would sometimes hear her comforting the newest baby as she nursed her to sleep—in the rocker.

With my own children, the rocker marked each child's passage from infancy to childhood; it belonged in the room of whichever child was currently "the baby," though occasionally it journeyed to another room, a source of comfort in severe illness. Nighttime nursings, quiet story-telling to calm an overactive toddler, soothing backrubs during midnight thunderstorms all went much better in the family rocker.

A few years into mothering, I visited my out-of-town sister, mother to two children at the time, discovering with dismay there was no rocker in her house. By some miracle, her children seemed happy and rested, they hugged and slept as well as mine, despite the glaring gap in their family's furniture.

So maybe it's not the rocker, I began to reason, not the piece of furniture, but the rhythm. Back and forth, at first quickly in tune with the baby's agitation, then more gently, always accompanied by lullabies or camp songs or sacred hymns. It's the same hypnotic rhythm as the waves brushing the lakeshore on a summer's night or the repetitious cooing of a mourning dove on the roof or the rhythmic fluid in a mother's womb.

Today, there's no "baby" in our home to lay claim to the family rocker, so it sits dormant near my bed gathering books and clothes and dust. Occasionally, my youngest dips back into her memory on a restless night by asking, "Just tonight, can you rock me in the rocker?" Gladly I agree, and we easily slip into the soothing rhythm that soon lulls us both to sleep.

ðŸ¦‹ TODAY: With or without a rocking chair, I'll hold my child a little longer, rocking to comfort us both.

So Much Noise

Then I heard what seemed to be the voice of a great multitude, like the sound of many waters and like the sound of mighty thunderpeals....—Revelation 19:6

THERE'S A LOT TO BE SAID for the contemplative life. Juliana of Norwich and Therese the Little Flower —they knew what they were doing. Take the noise level, for instance. The soft patter of nuns' feet scurrying into the refectory, the rustle of starched habits and the creak of chapel doors...little to intrude on their inner silence.

How different in the here and now of twentieth-century motherhood. I'm bombarded at every doorway by noise, rising in volume and pitch as the evening wears on. The muted tentative fumblings on the piano grow louder as my virtuoso gains confidence. My toddler, grimy fingers clutching my skirt, babbles new sounds that mean little to me. Another, unpacking work from school, shouts above the others for my attention about papers that need to be signed and homework that needs supervision. In the background, the yelp of our persistent dog who's grown impatient waiting to be let outside.

Take time to center yourself, to focus on the inner quiet, advises a friend, a nun, whom I meet at a parish function. Mothers need that quiet, she reminds me. I nod my assent, wondering how many homes she's visited weekday evenings, when time is too short and each child believes the only way to get parents' attention is to outshout the others.

On rare occasions when the house is my own, I get in touch with pre-family sounds: the chirping of a cricket somewhere in the basement, the thump of the furnace periodically kicking on, the whirr of the refrigerator motor. I'd forgotten what an empty house "sounds" like...probably a lot like those cloisters of centuries ago. Too quiet, too empty. In truth, I'd never relinquish the clamor and the chaos I'm immersed in; it's too much a part of the family fabric. But...will someone please turn down the volume?!

🙠 TODAY: I will turn down the volume of nonhuman sounds, savoring the sounds of my family, matching each with the child who makes them.

Timely Matters

For everything there is a season, and a time for every matter under heaven.—Ecclesiastes 3:1

THEY'RE EVERYWHERE, from my rising to my lying down: clocks on coffeepots flashing "set me, set me" as I grope for filters and water, clocks on microwaves measuring exact seconds for the perfect bag of popcorn, clocks on four sides of city hall timing my "leisurely" lunch.

It wasn't always this way. Distant ancestors survived, and probably thrived, without clocks, preferring to measure life by days and seasons rather than microseconds. The cock crowed, and they roused themselves from bed to face the chores the day held. The sun rose overhead—time to leave the fields and break bread. Sundown, varying with the weather and the seasons, signalled the end of the day and a return to the security of the hearth.

For years, I resisted a wristwatch, trying to be in tune with my "inner clock," but with little success. I became a bother to colleagues, always snooping out the time from their watches, wondering which clock on the office wall was the "right" time. Realizing what a sham my attitude was, I gave in to convention. I now own two watches.

As a child, I don't remember being fixated with watches. Maybe they weren't the fashionable accessory they've become today; or maybe my life was less stressed than my own children's. Meetings, sports practices, favorite television shows all vie for their time, dividing their attention spans into artificial segments.

In this era, we need clocks and watches to be "on time." But we don't need to be their prisoners. The sun and the moon, the mourning dove and the nightingale, falling leaves and bursting buds—all tune us in to the rhythms of a time that is older and more enduring than any digital clock.

ಊ TODAY: I will resist the urge to constantly monitor the time. If I can't manage without my watch at work, I'll discard it as I walk in the door at home.

'...And to Dust You Shall Return'

...then the LORD God formed man from the dust of the ground, and breathed into his nostrils the breath of life....—Genesis 2:7

LET'S JUST SAY I'm in touch with my roots, my distant ancestors—Adam and Eve who were created out of dust. Dust bunnies under the beds, dust outlining the knick-knacks on my dresser, dust crusting over each slat of the miniblinds I haven't wiped since they were hung. The house is a nineties version of the "dust bowl."

It's not that dust doesn't bother me; it does, immensely. Dusting just isn't a priority in a life filled with children and other more essential tasks. Wiping immediate spills, sweeping layers of crumbs from linoleum and hardwood floors, cleaning toilets where germs might lurk, picking up clutter each night before bed—about all the housekeeping chores I can manage during a busy week. And, when company is on my doorstep, the dustrag goes into action...in the public parts of the house.

The bedrooms get neglected. What I need is a good old-fashioned spring cleaning like my mother used to do, I remind myself, come March. But by fall, the major cleaning still left untouched, the task seems almost insurmountable. So the dusting happens in spurts when some particular room cries out for attention. Perched on a chair to retrieve china from a remote shelf, I glance over the top of the refrigerator and attack it with soap and water. Adjusting the overhead fan from summer to winter settings, I swipe a layer or two of dust from the blades, taking at least some of it out of circulation for the season. One day, unable to concentrate on the more pressing intellectual tasks I've listed on my "to do" list, I attack the children's bedrooms, one at a time, leaving trails of dirtied rags in my path.

I'm not happy with my dust bin of a house, but it's a compromise I've made to spend the free time I do have with my family rather than being a slave to housework on weekends. I'm the one it bothers, not the children, who seem to take it in stride. Entering my bedroom, the dustiest in the house, one child complains of a sudden case of the sneezes.

"Maybe you're allergic to the dog—you're sitting near her favorite spot," I offer feebly.

"No, Mom," my youngest corrects me matter-of-factly, "I think it's the dust."

🐚 TODAY: We'll make dusting one room our realistic goal, and attack it as a family project.

Food Blues

Mom, sometime when I'm alive buy some good food.—Note found on refrigerator

CLEARLY MY EIGHT-YEAR-OLD is not happy. She has gone to the cupboard to get an after-school snack and found it bare...by her standards. Of course, the half-finished boxes of crackers, five varieties of cereal and a few pieces of assorted fruit don't count. She wants a good snack, and I have been remiss in providing it.

Obviously the problem boils down to a definition of terms: "good" and "food." I'm not a purist. As in most families, with my first child I had started on the straight-and-narrow nutrition road, avoiding chocolates and sugars in excess (until the pediatrician suggested she could put on some more weight and sweets might help). We've never been a pop-and-chips-in-the-hand family, but middle-of-the-roaders. I define ours as the "healthful but still fun" approach to eating.

But this end of the paycheck has been a little slim, so we're cruising by on leftover snacks that aren't meant to please but only to meet hunger needs; the storehouse is more depleted than usual.

Over the years the perennial question "Why don't you ever buy _____?" has brought a variety of answers from me, depending on my frame of mind. I try to avoid the classic "your plenty vs. the world's hunger" response, only because I had vowed I'd never use it on my children. I had never been impressed by it as a child, but now I understand what prompted my parents to challenge us with that answer: the real hunger in the world.

Will my children ever grasp the division between them and most of the children of the world? Only lately have I, as an adult, come to some appreciation of the gap. To my generation, starving children were only missionaries' anecdotes during Lenten appeals, symbolized by an emaciated African child reaching out toward me with his empty bowl. Today, though, we are linked instantaneously with children doomed to hunger from drought and floods, hurricanes and civil wars. My children should understand, but they've grown as insensitive to these repetitious electronic images as I had to the Lenten posters.

My children won't starve, despite their protests of nutritional neglect. I take some comfort as I reread my daughter's note so passionately penned for my benefit. She has thoughtfully reevaluated the extent of her hunger, scratching out from the corner of her original message a P.S. that reads, "You never bought good food since I was born." Passion tempered by reason—that's some cause for hope.

🐝 TODAY: I will be gentle in urging my children to eat well and to be grateful for the food with which they're blessed.

Mail Call

How beautiful upon the mountains are the feet of the messenger who announces peace, who brings good news,...—Isaiah 52:7

THE FREQUENT FIGHTS over who'll check the family mailbox often puzzle me: why fight over bulk rate circulars, utility bills, real estate notices of houses for sale? Every once in a while, one child will score a win, triumphantly displaying a family magazine we've subscribed to. But the anticipation is really a remnant of years gone by, when the mail was *the* way for people to stay in touch. Today, long distance calls and fax machines have rendered the mailbox almost antique.

Still, I relish the luxury of reading and re-reading a

letter or a postcard. A short note on a card from a beachfront vacation spot assures us that sisters and their children are enjoying the summer, despite sunburns, downpours and fire ants. A cryptic, yet meaty and sincere, note from Dad confirms that they will be down for Thanksgiving, and should they bring the pumpkin pies, as usual? A former business associate, an avid reader of the newspapers, sends along clippings we might enjoy, with a note bemoaning how little time we have to visit.

Then there's the special mail, the keepers. A handwritten note from a dear friend, thanking us for a dinner at our home (children included, not on their best behavior), affirming us for our efforts at the tough task of modern parenting. A newsy letter from Mom, who still takes time to write, in addition to our periodic phone calls. Her letters are real "visits": They update me on classmates long-forgotten, remind me of an uncle's birthday or upcoming surgery, chat about strawberries she's picked or tomatoes she's canned for the winter. And always, a special message to her grandchildren.

They, too, must sense, as young and modern as they are, the special treat of a letter from someone loved. So, despite their too-frequent disappointment after emptying the mailbox, and the cries of "How come no one ever writes *me*?" they hold out hope that someday ("How about if I write first?") that junk-filled mailbox will hold a treasure just for them, one they'll savor longer than a dozen phone calls.

🐾 TODAY: I will take time to write a letter, no matter how brief, to a friend or relative who's been lately on my mind and in my heart.

Pondering the Depths

Mom, where do birds go during a tornado?
—Liz Barkley, age 8

MOMS—THEY HAVE ALL the answers. Sure. If their children didn't keep coming up with new, unanswerable questions.

"What's on television tonight?" "Where's the peanut butter?" "Have you seen my soccer shoes?" Those are the easy ones. But veer in the direction of philosophy, cosmology, theology, and I'm less certain.

Thank goodness for that uncertainty in my life, for questions from the deep, for the unfettered imaginations of my children. They send me scurrying to books for answers or, failing nearby and adequate resources, they challenge me to enter the world of fantasy they inhabit. With children, it's difficult to remain too straitlaced, too locked into the logical world. My children force me to look at the world from a new angle, anticipating their questions, absorbing their eagerness to discover more.

The humdrum "Yes" and "No" answers to workworld questions—"Is that report ready yet?" "Did you get the test results from the lab?"— pale next to the complexities of questions about the workings of thunder and lightning, the anatomy of crickets, the nature and number of angels.

Some of their questions—too heady, too earthy, too complicated—will have to wait for answers.

Q.: "Do I carry God in my heart all the time?"

A.: "Of course, God is always with you."
Q.: "Then when I drink milk, will God get wet?"

Yes, some questions are just too deep for a perplexed and amused mom.

❧ TODAY: I will share with my children a startling or surprising tidbit that I've read or overheard...before they can ask me another of their unanswerable questions.

Hard Work

By the sweat of your face you shall eat bread....
—Genesis 3:19

SOME TIME OFF. Time to watch late-night television, sleep late, do nothing. So how do I use my time? I work.

But it's a good work, a different kind of work—relaxing work. An oxymoron? Maybe, to those who really work for a living. But when's the last time I wiped sweat from my brow, aside from hot Saturdays at the pool? My job is people work, computer work, paperwork—a job my robust German ancestors would have puzzled over, furrowing their brows quizzically as they asked, "Vork?

You call dis Vork?"

I put on my oldest T-shirt and my jeans worn at the knees to meet my friends at their new home. A nighttime rendezvous after our children are in bed—to scrape and paint, to scrub and get dirty.

The painting is easy enough—just a little bending to reach the baseboards, producing a few cricks in the knees. Then we tackle the kitchen, three layers of dated wallpaper foiling us with much excess glue. The first layer had come off easily enough soaked in vinegar and water. But the next two prove more stubborn; with the assistance of a steamer, we scrape and peel and scrape some more, stretching to reach the high spots, testing arm and leg muscles long unused. The rugs are next, ground-in dirt forcing us to scrub and rinse then scrub again, until the liquid in the vacuum looks more like mud than water.

Long past midnight we call it quits, knowing one of us has an early morning flight to catch and two of us will be up early to rouse our children for school. Before leaving, we assess our progress—not dramatic, but enough to call our several hours' labor well worth it. We're weary, but proud.

Since our biblical parents were cast out of Eden with the admonition to work up a good sweat if they wanted to eat, we've taken a dim view of hard work: forced labor imposed by God, the just Enforcer. But this daughter of Eve finds physical labor more a reward than a punishment. Growing too moldy and flabby in my own work, I seek temporary fulfillment in scraping and scrubbing, dabbing and dumping, work with results more concrete and measurable than the way I earn my daily bread, and just as enriching when it's a labor of love for my friends.

❧ TODAY: I will find time to help a friend or neighbor with a small chore that may be physically too challenging for them.

Lost Weekends

And on the seventh day God finished the work he had done, and he rested on the seventh day from all the work that he had done.—Genesis 2:2

T HOSE WERE THE good Old Testament days, when a weary God could take Sunday off. "A mother's work is never done," my mother used to tell me. Even truer today than in the past, I'll venture. Weekends, once a slow-paced refuge from the workaday week, now blend in with Monday through Friday. But at least weekend "work" gives Saturday and Sunday a flavor all their own.

How long has it been since the floor has been really clean, not just wiped up after spills? Friday night seems the perfect time to get the long-neglected house in shape. Come Saturday morning, early, the buzz of activity begins. A crack-of-dawn trip to the grocery to stock the depleted cupboards and freezer. On the way home, we zip by the dry cleaners for shirts and suits. Then dance lessons, and between drop-off and pick-up times, we squeeze in a trip to the library to return long overdue books. The mall's open by now, so we dash in to exchange a pair of jeans. Home for a quick lunch and a brief respite, then it's off to soccer. Oops! No money left. Let's find a bank machine so we can fill the gas tank that's perilously near empty. A quiet dinner (carryout pizza to give the cook a break), baths, then bedtime. Half the weekend's gone.

Sunday morning. Whatever happened to those lazy hours lying in bed poring over a bulky newspaper and savoring a cup of coffee? The answer to my question tugs at my arm as I'm ready to roll over for my weekend's reward of an extra hour of sleep. Seven o'clock and my toddler is eager to play. Kiss that dream good-bye. Recalling what Sunday was meant to be, we're off to church after battles over the definition of "church clothes." Home again, lunch time, then the weekend's major challenge: laundry. Baskets full, accumulated from a week's worth of work and play. In between loads, we check school papers, help a shaky toddler down from the swing set, rake leaves or mow the lawn, supervise long-term school projects whose deadlines have arrived. Then it's dinner time, baths again, lunch-packing and off to bed.

"Did you have a relaxing weekend?" my colleagues are sure to ask Monday morning. Certain that they don't really want the truth, I'll nod a "yes" and smile a polite question in return, "And how about you?"

ঌ TODAY: I'll make time to sit still and relax this weekend by reading the paper, watching a lightweight TV show, or talking to a friend on the phone. I deserve it!

Sibling Harmony

I take pleasure in three things,
and they are beautiful in the sight of God
and of mortals:
agreement among brothers and sisters, friendship
among neighbors,
and a wife and a husband who live in harmony.
—Sirach 25:1

A MIRACLE WEEK—that's what we've decided to call the past seven days. No crutches piled at the front door, no manna raining down from the heavens...just a week of tranquillity among the children. Far from typical, especially with everyone home for a week, on break from work and school. More often, by day two or three the novelty of being together, of having free time, deteriorates into irritation and boredom. Then the bickering begins.

But somehow this week we've broken the pattern. Despite the age differences, the children have peacefully coexisted, even played as the best of friends. The middle child has temporarily abandoned her own bedrooom to move in with the youngest, preferring a fold-up cot and random blankets to the softness and security of her real bed. How long will this last, we wonder? They'll wake each other early and no one will get any rest. But the arrangement works, and we awaken to sounds of jabbering and laughter three mornings in a row.

"Check the address on the front of the house," my husband suggests, his wry humor mingling with wonder. What have we done wrong, or right, that we're living in such unexpected harmony? Is it the lack of stress in all of our lives because of much-needed vacations? Or have angels, knowing parents need a respite, temporarily inhabited the bodies of our children?

Even in travel, all of us squished in the car amid blankets, boots, pillows and books, the truce holds. A little friction over who's sitting where and I'm sure the peace has been shattered. I'm grateful to be disappointed. My tensed shoulders relax as I realize I won't have to slip into my mother-in-travel voice delivering the ultimatum, "If we have to stop the car, you won't be happy."

One day captures the charmed mood best. A picture-perfect fire brightens the house as we gather on couches and floor to relax, reading books or newspapers, playing board games whose rules we're still deciphering. Surely a "Norman Rockwell moment." Or perhaps a taste of the final reward that awaits us in our next—and happily, if this week is a foretaste—permanent life.

ﾠﾠ TODAY: When my children play peacefully together, I will affirm their behavior with praise.

A New Day Dawns

Create in me a clean heart, O God,
and put a new and right spirit within me.
Do not cast me away from your presence....
—Psalm 51:10-11

A STROKE OF DIVINE WISDOM that our lives are shaped by the rhythm of twenty-four-hour days: stressful days giving way to calmer nights, a time to give up the old day and begin again. At night, as I lie in bed before sleep takes over, I recall the day that's ended, often with more guilt than satisfaction. Why was I so curt, so impatient, so quick to blame? I chalk that day up as a loss for myself and for those I've touched.

But with the dawn, a gift from an ever-generous God: a day open to whatever I can bring to it.

The old, frigid heart of yesterday is forgotten; I ask for a "clean heart" today, one that is pure enough to see through externals that often mask the depth of the people I meet, one that won't judge motives, but merely accept the reality present to me.

Yesterday's defeated spirit, prone to discouragement and self-condemnation, is no more; in its place, I pray for "a new and right spirit": one that builds up rather than tears down—my spouse, my children, my coworkers; one that forgives my own failings even as it forgives those of others.

With morning, I can again believe that I walk in God's presence. I can't hope for it in a burning bush or a transfiguration upon a mountain or tongues of fire in an upper room. But I trust that it surrounds and protects me—as I begin the morning rituals of wakening weary children, reading the news, setting out to meet my daily world.

Each day is a gift in its newness. The God who created the world, who created morning and evening on that first day, continues that miracle each day through me, as I rise to greet the day and create my own little world anew.

&. TODAY: As I go to sleep tonight I will say a prayer of thanks for whatever this day has brought me, and remember to begin the new day with the resolution to accept my part in carrying out God's work of creation.

Living Day by Day

Do not boast about tomorrow,
for you do not know what a day may bring.
—Proverbs 27:1

MONTHLY SCHEDULES, calendars, long-range assignments, goals and objectives, five-year plans. My present life is shaped by plans for the future. Our culture has fostered this "looking ahead" frame of mind. I can reserve first-run videos a month early, open Christmas clubs at banks to save for gifts a year later, save for my children's college education before they finish kindergarten, select caskets and cemetery plots in anticipation of death.

But I never really know what tomorrow will bring. A weekend family getaway must be delayed when long-dreaded chicken pox finally breaks out in our home. Tickets to a touring Broadway play, ordered weeks in advance, get passed on to friends when a hospitalized relative needs care. An out-of-town conference, eagerly anticipated, eludes me as fog and ice ground scheduled airline flights.

Too often I want to be both creature and Creator, shaping the world to my plans, "boasting about tomorrow" when tomorrow is not mine to own. In a world controlled by deadlines and goals, it would be absurd to refuse to look toward the future. But sometimes "tomorrow" becomes an escape from looking at what the day can bring and what I can bring to the day.

One way I remind myself not to take the future so

seriously is to read each morning's obituaries. The 43-year-old hospital comptroller killed in a head-on collision, the 35-year-old civic leader dead of a heart attack, the family of four asphyxiated in their sleep—gruesome fare for breakfast reading, but a reality check for someone who counts too heavily on what tomorrow holds.

Rather than sanctifying the future with its unknown griefs or rewards, I need to cherish what Elizabeth Ann Seton called "the sacrament of the present moment." Too often the day at hand passes by in a blur, and I am deprived of the riches that it alone holds: that once-in-a-lifetime blend of people, hurts, joys and growth that will strengthen me to accept whatever the next days may bring.

~ TODAY: I will take time to say a short prayer of gratitude for today and ask to be open to the blessings and challenges it holds.

Parenting Goals

Never measure the height of a mountain, until
you have reached the top. Then you will see how low
it was.—Dag Hammarskjöld, Markings

WHAT DIVINE WISDOM that a baby must live for nine months in the uterus or that adoption procedures get complicated by on-again, off-again arrangements and bureaucratic paperwork delays. In the early stages of waiting, the thought of bearing, much less raising, a child overwhelms. "I know nothing about babies," a pregnant friend complains to me as her due date draws near. "Don't worry, no one does. But you'll learn."

After the initial realization that this wondrous newborn belongs to me, the challenges begin. "Newborns are easy. Wait till they become toddlers!" someone remarked to me early in my parenting life. Wearied from sleepless nights, fingers bearing scars of diaper pins that pierced me rather than the cloth on my baby's bottom, I smiled a grudging "thanks" and vowed never to give such advice to another unsuspecting parent.

On my own, I learned that each age brings unanticipated challenges: teething, weaning, wearisome trips up and down unprotected stairways to retrieve curious toddlers who can crawl up but not back down, wipeouts during trips on bikes without training wheels, heads wedged in wrought-iron porch railings, the first stitches, chicken pox (not simultaneous, of course, but week after wearying week). After conquering each step along the way, I was glad not to know what other surprises lay ahead.

As a child, I wished I could see into the future, just as my children wish now. "Who will die first—me or you?" my youngest wonders. They're fascinated by what will be as they grow older, spending hours creating, then interpreting, paper "cootie catchers" or "fortune tellers" that will predict new friends, career choices, travel plans, marriage details.

But for me, the present is enough. Wisely, my parents "kept all things in their hearts" about the heartaches of child-rearing. Now they seem serene, the immediacy of those challenges only a memory as they observe through grandparents' rose-colored lenses offspring grown and raising their own children. If I could have seen into the future, I might have turned away. Thankfully, we're creatures of the present, so that scaling the mountain of parenthood, the peak still out of sight, I try to focus on the "now" of the adventure. And I hope that once I reach that top, I'll see how low that mountain really was.

❧ TODAY: When I become overwhelmed by the challenges of raising my children, I'll say a prayer for the grace to take one step at a time toward the summit of this seemingly endless mountain.

Waiting for the Light

By the tender mercy of our God,
  the dawn from on high will break upon us,
to give light to those who sit in darkness and in the
    shadow of death,
  to guide our feet into the way of peace.—Luke 1:78-79

THE CRISP PAPER SONGBOOKS lying in the pews and the oversized Advent wreath mark the beginning of a new liturgical season. The readings, the songs, the homily all remind me to prepare for the Lord's coming, to wait for the light of Christmas morn.

But right now I'm engulfed in darkness more than light. I know how I should feel: calm, silent, eager for Christmas day. But my real feelings dominate: gloom over plans not made, gifts not bought, cards not addressed or written. As a child, the month of December would drag, each day marked off on the Advent calendar as one less to wait for midnight Mass, then the thrill of Christmas morning; now the days rush by in a blur.

My parish offers me help: family get-togethers to create Advent wreaths, evening reflections on Advent readings, pep talks about keeping the true spirit of the season. But I have no time and little energy for "the true spirit."

And it's not just the "buy-buy-buy" messages I'm immersed in that zap my strength. My weeks are crammed with "legitimate" projects in the true spirit of Christmas: shopping for food for an elderly lady who lives alone, buying gifts for the children's adopted poor families at school, lifting tags from the parish "giving tree" to supply Christmas gifts for area needy. I choose involvement to help my children understand that Christmas is giving. But often the giving is there without the spirit of giving.

I'm waiting not in despair, but in darkness, looking for someone to "guide my feet in the way of peace." I love the shopping, the wrapping, the giving, the music of the Advent season, the anticipation in my own children's eyes. But my feet grow weary tramping through malls and waiting in lines. Since I can't shed the commitments already made, I resolve to take advantage of the built-in moments of reflection, time already committed to Sunday Mass. Then, come Christmas, I may not experience the joys of a full-fledged "dawn from on high," but at least I'll be able to share in some of the light promised to those sitting in darkness.

❧ TODAY: At Sunday liturgy I will focus on Advent by really listening to the Word of God, singing with conviction the songs of the Mass, and savoring the message of each homily.

Saying 'No'

Just say no!—Drug education slogan

I
T'S NOT DRUGS or alcohol or even tobacco, but it's an
addiction nonetheless, one that has me in its
clutches: I'm a compulsive "yes-woman."
It's a subtle habit, one that masks itself as a desire to
help those in need. And partially that's what motivates
me. Requests bombard me from all sides: to serve on
parish commissions, to collect donations for worthy
causes, to lead Scout troops, to author articles. The
onslaught is dizzying and gratifying. Someone out there
can't do without me.

One part of me is noble—worrying that a program
might be canceled from lack of interest, hoping an event
will make enough money for those suffering hardship,
wishing for my children the joys of being on a team with
an energetic leader.

But other less exalted motives emerge as I examine the
whys of overcommitment. Serving on that particular
board will enhance my resume. How can I turn down a
chance to write for such a prestigious publication? Surely
I'll go down in local history as a "supermom" if I can
tackle that volunteer job in addition to my own career.
And, almost childish: Will they still like me if I say "no"?

A friend, sharing her own wish to extricate herself
from the web of overcommitment, spills out her
frustration at lack of time with her children. I listen,
encouraging her to cut back. Later, as I analyze her to my
husband ("Her problem is she needs to learn to say

'no' "), his widened eyes and on-target remark startle me: "You're no one to talk."

So, I vow to cut back, to focus my talents and my "yesses" so I can be more available for my family, who see too little of me as it is. The first "no" is tentative but not too difficult: Could I help out with an upcoming workshop by heading the publicity effort? Coming from an acquaintance, not a friend, the request is easy enough to deny. Soon after, a phone call from a boss looking for "thoughtful people" like me for a high-profile committee— and my resolve weakens. Will it look bad for me? Will he think me uncommitted? I summon up courage, then mutter a hesitant "no, thanks, I have more committees than I can handle right now."

Those first rejections over, I feel freer, though still busy enough to shed even more responsibilities. Now, not all my responses are "no." I still utter an occasional "yes," but these "yesses" are now real choices.

❧ TODAY: I will examine commitments beyond family and career to see where I can cut back to allow more time for the essentials in my life.

Helping Out

Contribute to the needs of the saints; extend hospitality to strangers.—Romans 12:13

"**N**O MORE!" my already-crammed calendar seems to scream at me as I pencil yet another meeting onto its overflowing lines. Yet I argue, "Other meetings are expendable, but not this one."

There's no earthly reason to attend: no pay, no glory, not even decent refreshments. Just a chance to serve others in need. With a little creativity, I could find plenty of excuses not to go—I'm tired from long days at work, there are no clean clothes in the house, someone else is more talented. Hey, folks, don't look to me for help—I'm a "working mom"! But what mom isn't?

With many moms working for pay outside these days, it's easy to dismiss volunteer efforts as outdated or outmoded. It's a dangerous mindset, one that I find myself slipping into as I'm bombarded by appeal after appeal to serve on parish committees, organize fleamarkets, lead Scout troops, or supervise car washes for the school booster club.

I can't do any more. Not true. More correctly, I can't do it all. No one can; that's why I must do my part. I'll share the work with lots of others: moms and dads whose talents will be lost to our community if they burn out from overload.

I can type one more newsletter, cut one more set of pumpkin patterns, bake one more batch of brownies (the ten-minute microwave version, but who will know?).

Little by little, the "needs of the saints" will be served, the Body of Christ will be nourished by the talents of its eyes, ears, fingers and heart working together. And my children will learn, without my preaching it, that sometimes the best things in life are done for free.

🙠 TODAY: I will survey my talents and my calendar to see in what small way my volunteer efforts can enrich others without taking too great a toll on my family.

Preserving the Temple

For God's temple is holy, and you are that temple.
—1 Corinthians 3:17b

T HIS WORN-OUT, DRAGGED-DOWN BODY God's temple? Surely, this is Paul at his tongue-in-cheek best. Perhaps remnants of a temple unearthed in an archaeological dig, but not an example of God's creative architecture.

Sitting in the pediatrician's office, I thumb casually through magazines that offer a variety of recipes for preserving my body's youth. They celebrate the wonders of facials and massages, exercises to flatten tummies and loosen tight necks, power walking and mind-stretching yoga. I chuckle quietly to myself as I cuddle my sick child—who has time to read about these miracle cures, much less try them?

"Just Ten Minutes a Day—and You'll Feel Like a New Woman!" the headlines promise. I vow to exercise every morning, but after three nighttime trips to children's bedrooms, the extra ten minutes on my hardly-mussed pillow seem too inviting. Nightly strolls around the block look easy enough, but evenings, before darkness sets in, there are dishes to wash, homework to check, lunches to pack.

"Join an aerobics class, just two nights a week," my single friend urges. And I'm caught in a dilemma: preserve my health so I can be a better, more vibrant mother, or spend what little "free" time I have with my children.

I know there is no easy way, so compromise must win out. Take a ten-minute walk at lunch (forget about catching up on work those extra minutes). Get an exercise video and make renewing my crumbling temple a family affair. Start with five minutes of stretching and situps each morning, reserving the other five for extra sleep.

No matter how others see it, my body is precious in the sight of the Lord. No holy temple should remain in such a state of disrepair. My next priority project: bigtime temple restoration.

֍ TODAY: I will map out a realistic and achievable plan to work exercise into my already busy life. I'll try it for at least two weeks before getting discouraged.

Teary-eyed

...he will wipe every tear from their eyes.
—*Revelation 21:4*

FORTUNATELY THEY'RE KIND, or the epithet "crybaby" would come flying out in a chorus of jeers all too often. But after their initial wonder at this creature whose eyes brim over with little provocation, my children have come to accept me for what I am: a weepy mother.

No comely Michelangelo Pieta am I, just a down-home sort of sobber. I do give myself credit for attempting at one time to be subtle. But all decorum vanished once my children caught on to my crying ways. When they were young, I had the luxury of viewing an emotional movie undisturbed, tears spontaneously welling up in my eyes just at the dramatic high point. Ever-so-quietly I'd raise a tissue to pat them dry.

By now, however, I've been stripped of any remaining dignity. As the music crescendos to signal an approaching crisis on screen, three heads turn toward me to check out my eyes. "Oh, no, Mom's gonna start crying again." And they wait. Sometimes, eager to foil their smug predictions, I shift from being sentimental to being plain defiant. Other times, I give in to my weeping urge, despite their snickers.

"Why do you cry all the time?" they wonder when "it's just a movie" or "just a song." Self-analysis reveals several failproof tear-triggers: scenes of family unity after crisis, or poignant testimonials of love. Christmastime sets me off too—not just time-honored classic Christmas films, but almost any song, especially ones I remember singing in a choir at Midnight Mass. Add to these occasions most infant baptisms, though by now I've steeled myself so as not to make a scene in the second row of church pews with three pairs of eyes riveted on mine to monitor and publicly note the first drops. Any performance by any one of my children is also a sure trigger: Scripture readings at a children's liturgy, a piano solo, a holiday ballet for residents of a nursing home (that one's truly failproof with its combination of the young and the old).

Why do I cry? Chalk it up to hormones or vulnerability from lack of sleep or a keen mind that sees relations between the fictional and the real. My children don't understand now, but I know they will, once they're parents...unless there's a backlash to atone for the sentimental sins of their mother. But I'm holding out hope; I feel confident that in the end my crying genes will prevail to dominate at least one of the next generation.

ੴ TODAY: I'll allow myself the luxury of a cathartic cry by reading a favorite Scripture passage or poem or by listening to a particularly moving song.

Winding Down

Be still, and know that I am God.—Psalm 46:10

THE AGENDA FOR A MOTHER'S DAY is hardly Olympic material, but it's demanding enough to win her a medal for endurance and perpetual motion.

Mothers, take your mark. The alarm buzzes and ... they're off. Plug in the coffeepot and the curling iron. Into the shower, then out. Now the first round of the most demanding morning event—child-waking, a challenge fraught with dangers for the partipant chasing the elusive gold medal.

Cook breakfast, hurl the dishes into the sink. Next event—the morning triathalon of tying shoes, buttoning coats, retrieving lost lunches. Over the obstacle course of ballet shoes, library books and headless dinosaurs, into the car and the menace of the freeway. A day at work, then a deep breath as the trip home begins.

No wonder my physical and mental muscles ache by day's end. Except for quick bathroom breaks, when do I sit down and sit still? Passing elderly neighbors rocking serenely on front porches, I wonder what I would do with an hour of quiet. Always there are chores to do—one more load of laundry, one more phone call to return, one more school assignment to check.

The frenzied pace of modern life is the norm, but it's not natural. How can I stay in touch with the world around me if it's blurred as I run past it? How can I tap into the reservoir of my own inner strength if the motion of my busyness sends waves into those still, interior waters?

Never will I be able to complete every chore on my long "things to do today" list. Never will I be able to return every phone call as quickly as the caller demands. I need to sit still, set my priorities straight. A few moments to be energized and revitalized, to remember who I am and why I've chosen to live my days in the "fast forward" mode. Surely I can find five minutes out of twenty-four hours: a little stillness goes a long way.

❧ TODAY: I will take five or ten minutes that I think I don't have to turn off the noises of daily life. I will sit still and allow the quiet to touch me before I launch into my next task.

The Creative Word

*In the beginning was the Word, and the Word was with
God, and the Word was God.—John 1:1*

IN THE BEGINNING they have no words, only the
inarticulate utterings of newborns, sounds that we
so desperately want to attach meaning to, sounds
translated and written as "coo" and "ga-ga." We give
them their words, just as our words were given to us. At
the first "da," we fuss and coo ourselves, noting the date
of the utterance on calendars and memory books under
"baby's first word." Was it really a "word," a sound with
meaning? Possibly not, but we assign intention...and real
"words" follow.

Our excitement at the first word diminishes as we
begin to take our children's language for granted. Sounds
close enough to the actual words "bottle" (baa-baa) and
"blanket" ("banky," even "ginky") slip into our adult
vocabulary as we grow accustomed to this miracle of
communication. Often frustration and irritation
dominate, completely blurring our original wonder.

"What do you want?" I find myself muttering in frustration over a two-year-old's requests that are incomprehensible but persistent. Finally, the word fails, and we resort to a multiple-choice system of questioning: "This?" No. "This?" No. "Oh, thi-is? That's what you want?"

Eventually toddler chatter becomes so much a part of our routine that I tune out the words, hearing only a drone of conversation in the back seat above the drone of the car's motor. I'm too immersed in my inner world of words to hear the words around me— until I'm called back by the accusatory "Mommy, listen!"

What has become of my reverence for the first words, for their ability to give life? In essence tuned out to their words, I pretend to carry on "conversations" with my children, without turning off vacuums or televisions or dishwashers. How can I begin to understand their words if I can't even hear them over the din?

I need to rediscover the power of words, to model my words more closely on the creativity of the original Word. In a culture permeated with meaningless words, seductive words, this won't be easy. But in making contact with my children at their deepest level, I'll be moving back to the creative and redemptive intent of the original Word, the "Logos," and my words will simply be another affirmation of the primal and eternal "I love you."

❧ TODAY: When my children speak to me, I will try to listen to their words and the feelings behind them, encouraging them to continue until I understand what they really mean.

Celebrating the 'Firsts' of Life

You have a long road to travel before you,
And tying your shoe is only the first tying.
—Maire Mhac an tSaoi, "The First Shoe"

H OW MANY FIRSTS they master and how casually
I sometimes view these accomplishments.
I celebrated the firsts of my firstborn so
permanently, on a calendar of Baby's First Year. "First
rolled over," "First solid food," "First word." At eleven,
she still loves to flip through that calendar, trying to
remember those milestones.

But the firsts of my other children have been
swallowed up by the urgency of day-to-day matters.
They, too, tied shoes the first time, maybe to the applause
only of older siblings who affirmed the coordination and
concentration such a seemingly routine task really
demands.

Even as they grow, our children look upon firsts as an
important part of life. "So what's new?" is a casual
greeting we never think about. To children, everything's
new: climbing that first step (and we scold, lest they fall),
sounding out a word for the first time, riding down the
driveway on a two-wheeler without training wheels,
writing a list of spelling words in cursive penmanship,
mastering the stick shift on a car (so what if the gears
grind just a little?).

When we adults face firsts, what massive productions
we make of them: the first struggle with a new computer
program, the first successful transaction at an automatic

teller machine, the first research paper in an evening college class.

I miss some of the wonder of life, the newness of life, when I fail to notice the firsts of my children's lives (and my own). With everything new under the sun, affirmation and celebration should be the order of every day.

ঽ TODAY: I will take time to notice some "first" my children are struggling with, and applaud them, even if they fail.

Picturebook Memories

I was a child once, I know it; my mother has pictures to show it, but she always knew I'd outgrow it; I guess that's what pictures are for.—Erich Sylvester, "Stay With Me"

THERE THEY SIT—casualties of my busy schedule— four envelopes of photographs, how many months old by now I can't say for sure. They nag at me, reminding me of my promise not to let them pile up as my parents did, so that sorting through boxes of unlabeled pictures has become a task of their retirement.

Already my sisters and I have called dibs on particular family photos we'll keep as heirlooms. Already some have been reproduced and given out as Christmas gifts—classic black and whites from our own childhood. I suspect my own children will exchange similar gifts some day.

On rainy days or when they tire of puzzles and coloring, they ask me to retrieve from the high closet shelf their favorite albums ("the ones with me as a baby"). Sometimes I break from household tasks to remember along with them. Here's my oldest as a newborn, weighing in to the world at five and a half pounds, "little frog legs," hardly filling her aunt's strong hands. More babies, more pictures documenting each one's growth. Another of my first child, now the big sister in her shirt proclaiming that message, cradling her baby sister safely against couch pillows. Then the two of them, now "big girl" toddlers, in the hospital room, sitting on the high bed—three girls and their mom.

School photographs, too, record the amazing transformations of each year as we lay them side by side, commenting on changes in hairstyles, lost teeth, the onset of glasses and braces, the wide-eyed full grins of children changing to the whimsical smiles of almost-teens. "Remember that dress? I loved it!" exclaims my middle child, pointing out the same outfit in portraits from two years in a row.

For the youngest, pictures are a tenuous link with her roots, the home she left when she was on the verge of walking. Though we drive by the house occasionally, the older children reminding her of forgotten details, she "remembers" most of that early life only from photo albums: beds now separated that were bunk beds then, the homemade sandbox in the corner of the fenced backyard, the wrought-iron porch railing where her big sister's head was lodged so securely that the fire department was called to set her free.

Better than videos which move too quickly through parades, birthday parties or walks along the lake, picture albums are perfectly matched with young minds, keeping pace with their fertile imaginations. Curling up on a bed with a stack of albums—what a great way to "waste" an afternoon, savoring the magic of childhood days whose memories are too precious to forget.

🐾 TODAY: I will sort through and label at least one pack of piled-up pictures lest the task loom so large that I never dare to tackle it.

In Fear and Trembling

And some, for a child's sake,
Anticipating doom,
Empty the world to make
The world safe as a room.
—Louis Simpson, "The Goodnight"

DOWN THE STREET, sirens scream as emergency vehicles round the bend to our neighborhood. I freeze, trying not to think the unthinkable, and take a quick inventory of my children: one upstairs, one at Scouts, one riding bikes with a friend. The last realization spurs me to the door, and I breathe less rapidly as I watch them steering their bikes toward home.

Nerve-wracking, this job of parenting. Everywhere from infancy to young adulthood harm seems to stalk my children. In the crib, toys one day thought safe, the next day are recalled for defects. At the park, unfamiliar adults could be the "strangers" children learn they must fear. In the schoolyard and at malls, a drug dealer passes as just another kid—how can we really expect them to "just say no" when they're out from under our protective wings?

Enough! This will drive me crazy. This "danger lurking behind every rock" view of life isn't healthy...for parent or child. It leads to a tamperproof, greenhouse life for children, with built-in controls everywhere to cramp their physical, social and emotional growth.

I'm not the first mother, and won't be the last, to think the world too treacherous for children. But mothers before me have unlocked the protective doors of their homes and their hearts to let their children explore the wider world...into the woods of the frontier to climb trees, turn over rocks, wade in streams bulging from spring rains; on dates in cars of the thirties and forties that were death traps compared with today's; to swimming holes for relief from unairconditioned houses.

Another mother, Mary of Nazareth, also feared for her son as he wandered among the learned men in temples...lost to her and Joseph, but in touch with himself. Letting go means letting them grow and live, and really believing in a providential God.

🐦 TODAY: When I catch myself saying no to my children's activities, I will step back to evaluate whether I'm being sensibly cautious or just neurotic.

A New School Year

...you shall have to clear out the old to make way for the new.—Leviticus 26:10

I T'S A WAITING GAME, a challenge to parents' patience. The present is no longer of interest to them, only this day in the future, the first day of school. For weeks they've been sorting through clothes to find what fits...current sizes and current fashions. Which pants, which hair bows, which shoes—crucial decisions as the days lumber by at a tedious pace.

The days grow longer, with nothing satisfying their end-of-summer boredom: not swimming, not reading, not yet-another-rerun of last season's favorite shows. The summer has grown stale.

Finally, the night before school arrives; it's hard for them to sit still. Already they've memorized class lists posted in the school auditorium. It's not that they're so eager to work again—summer has made them lazy and slow-paced—it's the newness and anticipation. It's old friends they've seen only sporadically for three months, and new students whose names on homeroom lists have piqued their interest. What will teachers be like? Rumors fly: She's mean, he's fun, math tests are a pain. Each is an expert to younger children hungry to begin.

The little ones—what will the first day be like for them? "I'm scared, Mom. Kindergarten was fun. First grade will be so hard. What if no one likes me?"

The older ones—they're not the same children who fled classrooms last June. Old friends—will they still be friends? Will teachers acknowledge the summer's growth and changes, or will they cling to old images and labels?

Questions, anxieties, excitement. "I can't get to sleep, it's like the night before Christmas," my oldest complains on her third trip downstairs.

And it is. Awaiting them are unknown gifts in colorful and enticing wrappings: the richness, the newness, the surprises of another first day of school.

❧ TODAY: I will celebrate the first day of the school year with a special treat, a back-to-school dinner or a "Happy New Year" party.

Clothed in Memories

For everything there is a season, and a time for every matter under heaven:...a time to keep, and a time to throw away.—Ecclesiastes 3:1, 6

IT'S THAT TIME AGAIN: my semiannual trip to the storage room to sort through bags of clothes my children have outgrown. This trip has been prompted by a phone call to a sister out of town. She tells me how quickly her youngest has grown in the four months since we've seen her. Time to dig through clothes and dig up memories, releasing both in this cathartic ritual.

How durable these tiny outfits are. Sure, some are spotted with baby food or marker (the indelible kind I try to keep out of the reach of tiny artistic hands). But most are still wearable for romping around with no special place to go. My youngest, bored because the older children are engrossed in a too-complex game, accompanies me on my sentimental journey. She, of course, has been the latest to wear most of what we're about to part with, unless she was the wrong size in the wrong season. Like me, she wants to hold on to the past, protesting that a favorite sweatsuit (the red velour one, a gift from a grandmother) still fits—until she holds it against her sprouting body and we laugh at such a silly notion.

"Oh, I remember that one!" she exclaims, as we dig deeper into the mound of sweatshirts and dresses. "That was my favorite" she repeats about several others, unwilling to narrow her choices down to real favorites.

For me, the memories go deeper. I remember her in this dress, these overalls, and I remember her older sisters too. Those flowered jeans—a gift from friends at the second child's baptism. How many photos they appear in as they've been passed down, borrowed by neighbors, then returned for our youngest. That sweater— cashmere, no less—a gift from a godfather, unmarried and childless then, traveling through Europe. Those dreaded words, "Dry clean only," kept it more on the shelf than on the children. A striped shirt and matching pants—no designer labels, but the outfit is etched in my memory by a picture of our oldest "reading" at age ten months on her grandfather's lap shortly before he died.

Bittersweet, the memories that rush through me as I fold outgrown clothes neatly in a box for mailing. The sensible me wants to pass them on for yet another cycle of wear; but the sentimental me yearns to return them to the dark safety of tied plastic bags. It's not the clothes that I cling to, but the past—infancy and toddler years now over. Predictably, my practical urges win out, but not without a little struggle and a few regrets. The clothes may soon be gone, but I'll always be grateful for this afternoon of savoring their memories.

&❧ TODAY: I will sort through old clothes my children can no longer wear and find a relative, neighbor or needy child to share them with.

The Task of Learning

*Apply your mind to instruction
and your ear to words of knowledge.—Proverbs 23:12*

EVERY PARENT NEEDS the experience of going back to school: Learn a new language, take Statistics 101, master a new piece of high-tech equipment (one unrelated to anything you've ever operated before). Then begin to understand the challenges of your children's lives.

Take reading. I don't remember never being able not to read—it's always been a basic assumption of life. I do remember some stories from second-grade readers (in those days it really was Dick and Jane and Spot), but what about that moment when the process of reading finally took hold? Was I as frustrated as my children when they first approach the abstractions of sound and meaning connected with printed signs on a page? "Just sound it out!" their siblings encourage them, so they rummage through their memories to connect sounds with letters—short or long? hard or soft? So many words look alike ("was" or "saw," "dig" or "did") that the letters crowd in on their already-overloaded memories.

Another challenge: math. How to get past the "counters" and fingers to memorize the basic facts? We drill and drill until the flash cards become ragged; slowly we make progress until all that's foggy are the nines times tables and a few of the eights. (8 x 7 and 9 x 6 always gave me trouble too. Maybe it's a genetic defect.)

Last year when I spent some time studying Spanish, I

relived the frustrations and hard work of learning from scratch. At my age, with logic in ascendency but memory fading, the task of memorizing vocabulary and word endings almost did me in. Homemade Spanish-to-English flash cards became an appendage, and on trips to work, Spanish on cassettes replaced the morning news.

"This is too frustrating!" my youngest often exclaims in exasperation, unable to make correct change or tell time or learn addition facts. In the past, with the older children, I assumed they'd just "get it," so I pushed them with little sympathy to "Keep trying."

Now, somewhat humbled by my return to the ranks of student, I keep before me the image of my kind and oh-so-patient teacher (fluent in English and Spanish and Portuguese) leading her novice student along with praise. I applaud my children's smallest triumphs, encourage sticking with the task, and know that if we plod along together, soon "this too shall pass."

❧ TODAY: I will reward my children with lavish praise when they try particularly hard to master a new skill.

Guileless

'Tis a gift to be simple, 'tis a gift to be free...—Shaker Song, "Simple Gifts"

IS THE EXPRESSION ON HER FACE the shock of pride or the shock of incredulity, I wonder as the first-grade teacher meets me in the hall. She wants to show me my child's math test. Finally, I breathe to myself, my child has passed that timed test on facts from one to ten. For weeks the test has been the albatross around our necks. Seventy problems in five minutes—not an impossible task for six-year-olds...if they'd just stop trying to use their fingers as counters and work with flash cards.

At the teacher's advice, I'd copied the test multiple times so we could practice at home. She was making progress: from 24/70 to 54/70. And the home test the night before had been nearly perfect. Finally, we can put the flash cards away, I conclude, as I look eagerly at the test thrust under my eyes, searching for a 100% to confirm my hopes.

But no grade at all. And with a gasp of recognition, I notice the telltale signs of liquid correction fluid covering old dates and old errors. My daughter, my innocent child, had substituted her test from home for the one administered in school that day. Disbelief, then embarrassment, then guilt for pushing her so hard sweep over me. Yes, please confront her, I say to the teacher, and we'll talk to her at home. After school, I call her to my side out of the earshot of her siblings. At the mention of the math test, she crumples into my arms, eyes downcast, shoulders shaking from her sobs. I apologize for being so impatient with her in her efforts to learn, and explain that her punishment will be to write letters of apology to her teacher and her parents.

The letter brings tears to my eyes: "I am sorry I cheated. I hope you can forgive me." Without further fuss, we do and move on. My fears that we were raising a child with a devious, criminal mind are dispelled as I realize how childlike her first attempt at cheating has been. To her, the substitution was a clever way around an unpleasant task; to us, the deception was so transparent. Afraid that I had lost my baby to the wiles of a cheating world, I mutter a prayer of gratitude and smile with relief as she wonders wide-eyed about her teacher's wisdom, "But, Mom, how did she know?"

&amp#x2766; TODAY: I will encourage my children's honesty by accepting calmly any bad news they communicate (about spills, breaks, poor grades), rewarding their openness even when disapproving of their behavior.

Letter to Camp

For though absent in body, I am present in spirit....
—*1 Corinthians 5:3*

DEAR KATIE,
How was your first night at camp? I hope you slept well—that mattress didn't look too comfy. But you were probably so tired, it didn't bother you.

I thought about you last night, wondering how the food was, whether you'd made any new friends, if the raccoons came to visit your cabin. Mostly, though, my thoughts were thoughts of pride.

You were so excited—and a little anxious—on the trip up. When we walked into the tent with all those unfamiliar grownups, even I was a bit overwhelmed. But you answered their questions maturely, once in a while sneaking a glance to see if we were nearby.

Then as we moved on, you got a new spring in your step, leading the way over the hot, open field. As we sat down at the picnic table with your counselor, you made the break. No longer were we the all-knowing parents, protecting and talking about our child; now we were the bystanders, as you talked to her directly, person-to-person. Then I knew it was time for us to leave.

There's a saying to describe what happened yesterday at camp: It's called "cutting the apron strings." Think about that one. Many people feel it's harder for the child to let go of those strings, but after yesterday, I disagree. You did just fine. You kissed us good-bye, and in a flash, those apron strings were history.

You tease me because I cry at silly things, like sad movies and favorite hymns. Well, I admit, there are a few tears running down my cheeks as I write this. ("No offense, Mom, but that's really dumb.") You need to know they're not tears of sadness, but tears of pride in you, and a few for those useless "apron strings" I left lying in a heap at a camp miles away from home.

Miss you and love,

Mom

P.S. All right—rain! Finally you'll get to wear those klunky boots we trekked all over town to find.

⅔ TODAY: I will write notes to my children to let them know how proud I am of them—I'll send them via mail or their lunches.

Good-bye, Thumb

Not that I have already obtained this or reached the goal;
but I press on to make it my own....—Philippians 3:12

"I'M READY TO STOP sucking my thumb," my six-year old announces during Holy Week. Since this announcement is not unfamiliar, I try not to get too excited. When she's ready, she'll know, we've been told by our orthodontist—who's already ordered a second luxury car in anticipation of fitting her with braces sometime soon.

But today she seems serious, having pondered the rules of the bargain for several months: Thirty days in a row without sucking her thumb, then a prize at the end—mutually determined by her and her parents. The idea of a reward has been enticing, but weighed against loss of her thumb—comforter in times of distress and weariness—the decision to launch the withdrawal effort hasn't been easy.

When shall we begin? I suggest waiting until after the daylong trip to her grandmother's since there's not much to do for six hours in the car. But she's ready now. Off we go to the drugstore with her money (one of the rules) to purchase adhesive tape to wrap around her thumb, a concrete reminder of her pledge.

That first night challenges the whole family. Stories and back rubs—she's almost asleep—but then she's downstairs, whining that it's too hard. "Just hold onto your blankie," I suggest, but wisely she reminds me that the blanket is part of the ritual, and rubbing it only strengthens the urge to suck.

Friday's ride to our destination seems longer than usual to me, as I glance surreptitiously in the rearview mirror to note whether she's given up. Clutching a stuffed animal, she's sitting upright staring out the window, unable to sleep. As much as I want the thumb-sucking out of her life, I ache for her, a six-year-old only vaguely aware of the meaning of Good Friday, but in her childlike way mirroring the suffering Christ.

By day fifteen she's given up the tape—too much trouble—but her resolve is weakening. "I want to suck my thumb. This is too hard," she cries. "Don't give up now," I urge her. "You're halfway there."

When I check on her at night, I note her new position in the bed: In the past, she'd curled on her side, thumb in mouth, blanket in hand; now she lies on her back, arms and hands down at her sides, disciplined even in sleep.

Having forgotten to keep track as her thumbless life becomes routine, one day we check the calendar. The thirty days are up. (Forty, in fact, her own personal Lent during Eastertide.) Dropping everything, we drive to the store to purchase the reward she's finally named: a $2.99 set of petite press-on nails.

I am proud and tell her so, wondering if I could name and shed my addictions so courageously for so small a reward. Having reached her goal, she wears her trophy everywhere, symbol of her inner strength and her endurance.

🔊 TODAY: When my children make difficult decisions or stick to unpleasant tasks, I will affirm their strength with praise.

Growing Up

When I was a child, I spoke like a child, I thought like a child, I reasoned like a child; when I became an adult, I put an end to childish ways.—1 Corinthians 13:11

"THEY'RE ONLY LITTLE a short time. Before you know it they'll be all grown up," grandparents counseled me as I moaned about the cost of diapers, the inconvenience of car seats, sleepless nights with fussy toddlers.

And overnight it happened: My baby was no longer a baby. "Overnight," of course, is hyperbole, but the impact is the same. Just yesterday, I fixed her hair and chose her clothes; now my standards are too low. Not long ago I set the family fashion trends; now I'm challenged with "You're not going to wear that to the mall, are you?" Members of the opposite sex were a nonentity or at least a nuisance; now journals keep track of current infatuations and preteen heartbreaks.

My friends, also aghast at the rapid changes, report similar rumblings in their households. Thank goodness for more than one bath, they sigh, since their teenage boy showers two or three times a day...perhaps to cool down from the exertion of growing inches in months as he towers above his mother. One moment crystallizes this transformation from child to near-adult. For one friend, it's the day her boy began to shave, the fuzz visible enough to have to be dealt with. In our family, it's the onset of menstruation.

We weren't unprepared. In-school "family life"

instruction, met with giggles, seemed thorough enough. Then we spent a morning "for moms and daughters only" openly discussing anything from periods to PMS. Once her friends "started," she never left home unprepared, supplies camouflaged under sneakers and sweatshirts.

No intellectual or practical exercises could prepare me for the emotion of that day. She took it in stride, adapting to her new role gracefully. I'm the one still sorting through memories ("I began on a Girl Scout camping trip," I feel compelled to share with her) and feelings—a little wonder and a little fear. Will I be able to let go and let her grow into the woman her body says she's becoming? Despite the seesaw of emotions from day to day, she seems ready for her new role; I hope I'm ready for mine.

&. TODAY: Through an inside joke, a new responsibility or privilege, I will acknowledge approaching adulthood to my "child" who's rapidly becoming a young adult.

Leaving Their Mark

These days should be remembered and kept throughout every generation, in every family, province, and city....—Esther 9:28

EVER SINCE POURING THE CEMENT hours earlier to anchor the base of the new basketball hoop, we've drummed one message into the children's heads: Don't touch, it's still wet. Little wonder, then, that three small mouths gape in surprise as their father calls for a flashlight and a stick, urging "Hurry, let's write your names in it before it dries."

In darkness lit only by an arc of light, his three children huddled around him, he scratches the day's date into the still soggy base, then hands the stick to each child to write her name. One by one they meticulously create the perfect signature, while others advise with "Be sure to dot the *i*" and "No one's gonna be able to read that." If this is to be their legacy to future generations, it should be flawless.

By early morning their names have hardened into stone, indelible and unchanging. When we move on, their names will remain, a permanent reminder that the Barkleys had once lived and played at this address. But the marks my children will leave on the world beyond this home are still not drawn.

"What will I be when I grow up?"—this question plagues them constantly. As they mature, so do their dreams. Early on, they all aspire to be kindergarten and elementary teachers, modeling the energetic and caring teachers of their own school days. By middle school my oldest has already journeyed through a maze of career options: writer, musician and doctor rise to the top of her list most often, all boring choices to the youngest, who, at least for today, wants only to be a basketball player.

Of course, they'll be mothers too. This unspoken assumption underlies such vehement promises as "When I'm a mom I won't be so mean. I'll let my children play basketball even if it is dark" or shy questions like "Does it hurt a lot when you have a baby?"

As I watch my children confront the challenges of school and sports and the arts, I wish them the successes they already have hinted at during their brief lives, recorded in scrapbooks bulging with certificates of achievements, with ribbons from art shows and science fairs, with poems, short stories and newspaper clippings.

I hope to live long enough to bask in favorable reviews of their first novels or art shows or concerts, to sit in court chambers as one is sworn in as a judge, to applaud as another crosses the finish line in a marathon. But if none of these dreams becomes reality, if the world fails to single them out for public acclaim, I wish for them the "success" my parents wished for me—to make a mark on the world more enduring than a name engraved on plaques or trophies, the gentle impression made by a life of love and service.

இ TODAY: I will save something special my children create as a permanent reminder of the mark they've made on the world around them and on my life.

Adolescence

...it is the strangeness in the strangeness. It's the wonder of the wonder.—Henry James, "The Beast in the Jungle"

IT'S ENOUGH TO DRIVE A MOTHER CRAZY, this flitting in and out of adulthood called adolescence. Can't they just stay put—either in the land of children or the land of adults?

Not all cultures experience this ping-pong age, I've been told. A few initiation rites, a few ordeals to test their endurance, and—voila!—instant adult. The agony of growing up, for both child and parent, would pass quickly, rather than be spread mercilessly over the years. It's the unpredictability that's so nerve-wracking. Who am I dealing with today in this ever-changing body before me, child or adult?

Some days I'm convinced that we really haven't begun the journey toward adulthood, when she's more a child than her younger siblings—pulling hair just to aggravate them, flinging off a snide remark to detonate an already tumultuous evening, ignoring the toothbrush and the hairbrush in favor of the video game controls. Then she takes us all by surprise: "I'll buy the snacks with my babysitting money, Mom" or "Don't get up, let me put the dog out." Without prompting, she gives a glimpse of othercenteredness that I thought we'd never see. I catch my breath in wonder. Some days, braced for a typical response (or no response at all) to frequent requests for cooperation, I shudder at her ability to read my mind. "If I have to tell you one more time to make your bed...." "But, it's done. And I've brushed my teeth and picked up the bathroom too." Glimmers of hope and a promise of more surprises to come.

By next morning, though, she's reverted to former ways. Too much to hope for, this instant transformation. The surprise is that I'm still surprised. A friend with a son a few years older warns me, "Hold onto your hat—it's quite a ride." Never fond of roller coasters with their ups and downs, gravity-defying curves and terrifying heights, I wonder how I'll survive the adventure ahead. Too late now—I'm strapped in and on my way up the first stomach-churning hill. I could close my eyes and hold my breath to block out the terror. But I don't. Reluctantly, I release my white-knuckled hands from the restraining bar, as we near the crest before the first plunge. I vow to heed the advice of more seasoned parents who've been through the ride and are lining up for yet another thrill: "Let go and hang loose!" "Keep your eyes open—it's more fun." And..."Don't be afraid to scream."

❧ TODAY: I will make an effort to ignore insignificant externals that annoy me about my teenagers, trying to listen to the message they're communicating.

Creative Resume Writing

...to one he gave five talents, to another two, to another one, to each according to his ability.—Matthew 25:15

THE GLASS CEILING, the "mommy track." After years of putting off career advancement for more quality time with children, I'm ready to update my resume. Maybe "doctor" is a better word, as I try to use mothering experiences to my advancement. I flip through the most recent U.S. Department of Labor's *Occupational Outlook Handbook* to match my talents with titles for which I'm qualified.

Recreation workers. Who knows better than a mother that play is hard work? I've chaperoned roller-skating parties for second-graders with legs as wobbly as newborn Bambi's and taught frightened toddlers how to "make bubble faces" to learn to swim.

Psychologists. Sounds like my daily occupation. "Psyching them out"—that's the phrase they'd use to describe me as I calmly try to analyze what my child really means as she asks with a face wide-eyed with guilt, "Do you smell something funny?"

Flight attendants. "Mother is ready when you are" is my motto as I cheerfully help my disgruntled child pack to run away from home. "Write when you get work" and "Don't forget to brush your teeth."

Travel agents. Even if I haven't actually booked any cruises lately, I still know the best route to Grandma's, hitting only the fast food restaurants with outdoor playlands, motels with indoor pools and game rooms, and gas stations with unlocked restrooms to accommodate those unforseeable quick pit stops.

Police, detectives and special agents. I'm a Nancy Drew come of age as I unlock "The 7:30 a.m. Case of the Missing Sneaker," piece together "The Clues to the Chocolate Thumbprints" or unravel "The Mystery of the Disappearing Gerbil."

Dentists. No one could pay a professional dentist to sit through day after day of meals with a six-year-old wiggling a bloody tooth ("It really is loose, Mom!"). Subspecialty: Tooth Fairy, gently whisking precious teeth from under pillows and dispensing appropriate rewards.

Counselors. I've specialized in both academic and personal types, with heavy emphasis on grief counseling, when there are tears over breakups with best friends, goldfish lying belly-up in the bowl and tournaments lost to my slugger's inept fielding.

Roman Catholic priests. Of course, I'm a woman, but I'll plan ahead in case the winds of change sweep through the Vatican. No ordained priest has the practical theological experience I have in answering questions toddlers pose to me after a particularly long Sunday Mass, such as "Why didn't God ever show up?"

Roustabout. Roustabout? n. A laborer in a circus. My own childhood dream of freedom come true. After all I've been through with these kids, I deserve a break. Scrap that resume, I'm heading for the big top!

🐾 TODAY: I will take a few minutes of quiet time to reflect on how valuable my mothering experiences have been in my life beyond the family.

Maternal Strife

*The beginning of strife is like letting out water; so stop
before the quarrel breaks out.—Proverbs 17:14*

H OW CAN WE STOP THEM—these vitriolic
exchanges between "career moms" and "stay-at-
home moms"? Why do we line up and take
sides, pitting one against the other? "Divide and
conquer" is a good strategy, but usually it's division from
the outside, not from within.

I have a career beyond my family. I'm proud of it. My
husband's proud of it. For my children, it's a given,
though occasionally one will ask, "Why can't you stay at
home all the time, like so-and-so's mom?" It's a life we've
chosen, not without much weighing of values versus
drawbacks, just as many women have chosen to drop out
of the paid workforce to be at home full time.

Often our sniping at one another is unconscious, even
casual. "You work how many hours a week? And who
takes care of your children all that time?" "And what do
you do for a living? Oh, you don't have a job?"

The pain we inflict by such mean-spirited comments has always disturbed me, since I've been on both "sides" of the issue: for a while working evenings and some weekends or writing at home to have more time with our young children, then moving into my career full time as our children neared school age. But the pain of maternal putdowns hit me today when a friend shared her shock and hurt as she was summarily put in her place (in the home, with the children) by a thoughtless aside by a career-driven mother.

My friend, mother of four, is not unfamiliar with the business world. A clothing buyer with a major department store for many years, she gave up that career when her third child was born. Now she lovingly nurtures others' children in her home. The bruising words slipped from the lips of a mother picking up her children (late, as usual, creating havoc in the dinner hour of my friend's family).

"She was telling me about something she'd read in *Forbes*," my friend related to me. "Then she added, 'It's a business magazine,' as if she were explaining it to a child." Through this tagged-on comment, she had cruelly and falsely labeled my friend: You stay at home all day with children, how can you know anything about the intellectual world beyond these four walls?

Do our relations have to be adversarial? Can't we live in the spirit of the gospel where each of us is part of Christ's body, each different but essential? What's at stake and will any real winner emerge from this perpetual strife? I doubt it, but if so, you can bet it won't be our children.

& TODAY: I will carefully choose my words not only for their content but for negative nuances when I meet mothers whose lives have taken a different direction from mine.

Mean Mom

Train children in the right way,
and when old, they will not stray.—Proverbs 22:6

I KNEW THE WORDS would come echoing back to me before long, those words I heard from my parents time and again: "It hurts me more than it hurts you." The words inevitably accompanied the punishments that I already thought were excessive and undeserved, and that I promised myself I'd never impose on any of my children.

"Hurts" might not be the precise word, but it's close enough. Who really enjoys being disciplinarian, the most unpleasant of parents' diverse roles? I long for the easy way out, just letting them cruise by because "really they're not all that bad." And they're not *bad*, just lacking in the self-discipline and courtesy we'll expect when they're mature.

I know, they're just kids. But I've worked with too

many "kids" on the job whose maturity never caught up with their age. They're the ones who leave dirty dishes in the employee lounge—"Just carry your dishes over, rinse them and stack them in the dishwasher. What's the big deal?" They're the ones who stretch out already-long meetings because they haven't prepared beforehand— "You can't let your homework go until the last minute." They're the ones who snipe at coworkers, degrading them with caustic remarks—"Don't ever talk to your brother like that again, young lady!"

How much easier, especially at the end of a stressed-out day, to pick up the toys, close up the snacks and put them away, ignore the bickering. But it's an injustice, not only to my children, but to their future friends and spouses. I'd love to let them slip by—just relax, and forgo the dubious honor of being "the meanest mom in the world."

It's not a title I relish. I hope when they're calmer (or maybe when they're older), they'll forget the charges because the evidence doesn't match the crime. Besides, I seem to be in good company: My friends report that in their houses, they also reign as "the world's meanest mom."

❧ TODAY: I won't give up on reminding my children about inappropriate behavior, but I'll try to correct them out of love and with as much patience as possible.

Blowup

Refrain from anger, and forsake wrath.
Do not fret—it leads only to evil.—Psalm 37:8

I CAN FEEL IT COMING, but prediction does not equal prevention. My blood pressure jumps, my temper is short. I'm tired, they're tired. The perfect setting for a major blowup.

No one likes it, this explosion of anger that jolts the family, that wrenches the harmony we've worked so hard to achieve. I should walk away. Where to? I should take a deep breath. I do, but the children interpret this, with uncanny accuracy, as a sigh of exasperation. So the war of words begins.

Good parents don't scream at their children. That's the television image, that's the parenting book version. Intimidated by how we think we should act, we're slow to ask for sympathy and understanding from others. My younger sister, an innocent, phones in tears after losing her temper. "How could I have screamed like that? How could I have said those mean things to my own children?" But we do. Unless we're saints or living life in the tranquilizer lane, we lose it. No one comes out a winner.

It's comfortable to remember how Jesus got angry at the moneychangers in the temple. Righteous anger, we're counseled, is healthy. But this isn't righteous, it's trivial. The muddy soccer shoes piled in the corner since last week's game, the milk spilt on the just-cleaned kitchen floor, the bickering over favorite spots on the couch—

cause for anger? Hardly. Still, these are the catalysts after a stressful day, the sparks that ignite my short fuse.

Even as I berate them in words too strong for their offenses, I know I'm wrong, out of control. The angry words will linger, will haunt me as I hear them out of their mouths some later day.

Exchanging hugs amid tears, we make up, apologizing for words hurled angrily at those we truly love. A family rule—no one goes to bed in anger—brings calm at last. More resilient than I, they quickly fall asleep. And I, I lie awake restless, then steal in to check on them—so vulnerable, so fragile, so willing to accept my recommitment of motherly love.

🙰 TODAY: When I feel pushed to anger, I will take thirty seconds to pray for control. Should I lose my temper I will try to choose carefully the words I use. Should I fail in both, I will be the first to apologize.

Death of the Innocents

For these things I weep;
my eyes flow with tears;
for a comforter is far from me,
one to revive my courage.—Lamentations 1:16

T HE HEADLINE GRABS ME, drawing me into the story: "Families Mourn 5 Slain Nuns." I scan the first paragraphs and fumble for the jump story on an inside page, anxious to read the names; then I realize a distant connection with one of the dead. As the impact of the news sinks in, my sadness merges with indignation then anger. Five nuns, ministers of love and the "Good News," murdered, their small community's presence in a foreign country now erased.

Then, as if gravitating toward more of "man's inhumanity to man," my eye catches details of another slaying closer to home, equally inexplicable and senseless: a seven-year-old girl on her way to school shot by a sniper armed with a high-powered rifle—the third child from the same school killed this year.

Innocent nuns, innocent children— whether the deeds were deliberate or random, they reek of vileness. Earlier in life, I questioned the existence of evil, refusing to see sin as sin, instead opting for sociological or psychological explanations. How antiquated to suspect a devil lurking around every corner tempting people to sin, I scoffed. Today, more in touch with reality, I'm convinced of the existence of free will, with its obvious consequences: choosing good or choosing evil. How naive of me to think of devils only as Halloween caricatures with pitchforks, horns and tails.

The devil is alive and doing well, incarnated in power-hungry dictators or rebels (who knows the truth of conflicting accusations?) who gun down women in the service of God's people and in calculating snipers sighting down the barrels of sophisticated weapons to cut short three young lives.

In the wrong place, at the wrong time, my children are potential victims of evil out-of-control. Violent acts can kill their young bodies. But just growing up in a world permeated with evil can kill their young spirits. Short of loving them, warning them of evil and teaching them ways of peace, there's little I can do to shelter them from the violent among us.

&. TODAY: I will reread the famous peace prayer attributed to St. Francis of Assisi ("Lord, make me an instrument of your peace..."), trying to hear the words anew so I can incorporate some of his attitudes into my own life.

Abused

We are afflicted in every way, but not crushed;
perplexed, but not driven to despair; persecuted but not
forsaken; struck down, but not destroyed.
—*2 Corinthians 4:8-9*

THE DAMNING EVIDENCE is "as plain as the nose on her face," in fact, not far from the nose on her face: a large red abrasion bordering her right eye. Alone, it might be interpreted as an accident, a burn from a wayward curling iron, but not in combination with the reddened eyes and the distracted gaze.

I notice the mark mid-morning, but concerned with details of work that seem urgent, I tuck the observation away since I know her only by name, in passing. By early afternoon, though, I begin to struggle with what I should do. What if I embarrass her by prying? What if I embarrass myself in asking questions that imply violence when there has been none? Why should I presume to act as a counselor when I have no training as one? Finally, what if I don't ask and the abuse continues?

Nervous, unsure about how to begin, I sit next to her and begin tentatively with ice-breaking questions: "Are you OK?" "Did you have a rough night?" "Are you having trouble at home?" "Do you want to talk about it?" With each question, no firm response, but no rejection either, so I keep on, more confident that I'm on the right track. Then, without much emotion—no tears, as I had imagined—she reveals a little at a time in words that could have been lifted from a pamphlet entitled "Wife

Abuse: Classic Denial." "I should learn to keep my mouth shut. He's really pretty calm usually. He doesn't do it often. He always seems to pick a time when my son is in bed."

Now more angry than nervous, I try to formulate my reply without attacking her husband too directly: "No matter what you said, hitting you was not an appropriate response." Now that she has shared, will she seek help from someone trained to deal with these problems? To my surprise, yes. A quick cigarette and she follows me to a counselor—compliant, head down, as if she bears the blame for the abuse. As we walk, she's silent, relieved, but asks fearfully, "Will he have to know I told someone?"

"No one will know unless you tell them," I respond. Sadly, I realize this session marks not an end, but a beginning. Either she'll retreat to the former pattern— sealing the direction of her life—or she'll break away to suffer in a different way. As I entrust her to the care of professionals, I also utter a prayer that God will be with her in the pain that is sure to come.

ॐ TODAY: I will seek out a distressed coworker to offer support in her struggles, continuing to pray for God's healing in her life.

Power Play

Blessed are you when people revile you and persecute you....—Matthew 5:11

A S SOON AS HE SPEAKS the words, I can feel the heat rising slowly up my neck, tingeing my cheeks and ears in red. I had asked a question in innocence, to gain information; he had turned my question around to make me look foolish. His words are sharp and mean-spirited.

Publicly put down, I retreat to an inner cocoon to protect myself. I want to escape the room, but I remain in silent embarrassment until the group adjourns. Wondering whether my reaction is merely a function of fatigue and premenstrual hormones, I try to shake off my hurt. Then a colleague confirms my feelings: "He was out of line to talk to you that way." But since he is in a position of authority and I am not, he can have the last word.

So that's how it feels, I realize with a jolt and some guilt. That's what it's like to be a child, always the one without power, without authority, never allowed to have the last word in defense. As an adult—self-confident, successful, my personality already shaped—I will bounce back from the public shame. But what are children to do, unable to answer back, their emerging identities so fragile and vulnerable?

My own hurt still fresh, the recent words of my child ring painfully in my memory: "You embarrassed me in front of my friends." Unaware of the depth of feeling that accompanied the words, I'd brushed it off. Parents need to correct their children, I'd reasoned; maybe this will be one lesson not easily forgotten. But the real lesson might not be the intended one—about public behavior, appropriate language, responsibility. The real lesson ingrained in the child might be about power: Adults have it, you don't; when arguments reach an impasse, resort to power; your feelings don't matter, as long as I come out on top.

As adults dealing with adults, our power games are often subtly manipulative. With children, however, we're more direct in our need to control, no matter what the cost. Teacher to student, parent to child, too often our message to our children boils down to "Shut up and sit down." A sad message, one they'll carry within their hearts as they grow, surely not a message due any child of God at any age.

 è TODAY: When I catch myself speaking without respect for my child, I will change my tone to one that communicates reverence rather than dominance.

Nag, Nag, Nag

...do not provoke your children, or they may lose heart.—Colossians 3:21

"GET OFF MY BACK, Mom!"—my children's version of my childhood aversion to being "nagged" at. It's a fine nag-line I have to walk, and I plead guilty to crossing over one time too many. Somehow, I can't keep my perspective when it comes to living with my children's "unacceptable" personal habits.

What I need is a "nag scale," a measure from one to ten of the seriousness of their nonconformity to my standards. Personal hygiene would probably rank up near ten—washing hands, brushing teeth—since lack of compliance with standards can undermine health. Other "health" habits are somewhat harder to rank. Is washing and brushing hair related to health or to appearance? I waver. Probably a nine for washing and a five for brushing.

The distinctions become even fuzzier as I move to the next category, "Picking up toys and clothes." Too complex until I break it down further: Toys can be a hazard, especially tiny ones strewn on steps for someone to slip on or a baby to eat. Let's give that an eight. "Picking up clothes" presents another challenge: Where are they scattered? In public areas—I'll rank that five since they're in the way and often disgusting (especially foul-smelling socks stripped off after a sweaty ballgame). A week's worth of sweaters, shorts and socks piled on a bedroom chair pricks at my dominant compulsive side ("a place for everything, and everything in its place"), so I try to listen to the wisdom of my children, "Just close the door so you don't have to see it." My emotions argue for an eight on the scale, but logic puts this offense at about a three.

Next are environmental and economic issues: Closing the door on a winter day relates to both, so that's high on the nag scale, maybe a nine. Wasting food—a biggee—probably slips in around the same spot.

In truth, my children will never see this imaginary scale, but stepping outside the immediacy of the problems to categorize has been a useful exercise for me. The conventional advice, "pick your battles," reminds me to place these minor infractions within "the great scheme of things" in life, and think before I shriek about what, in the long run, is probably totally insignificant.

≈ TODAY: When I'm tempted to hound my children about their personal habits, I'll measure their "offenses" against my "nag scale" to determine whether to keep after them or to give them a little peace.

Sibling Battles

...they shall beat their swords into ploughshares and their spears into pruning hooks; nations shall not lift up sword against nation, neither shall they learn war any more.—Isaiah 2:4

NO MORE FIGHTING, no more wars. Surely a vision of the Kingdom, heavenly delights not known on earth, at least in our household. News of wars and skirmishes pepper the evening news, and I am sad. But wars just as real are fought daily in the battle zones on the homefront.

Most are turf wars. "She's sitting in my favorite place." "He wore my coat without asking." "It's my turn for the front seat." Insignificant in light of the blood shed through the ages, yet such skirmishes rival international conflicts in intensity, if not in scope.

First, the sniping: shoves, tongues thrust out in mockery, words aimed at vulnerable spots.

Next, attacks and counterattacks: "She called me a bad name." "Liar." "Tell him to stop looking at me."

Then the big guns, surface to air combat: toys hurled in anger, peanuts spit accurately across the dinner table when the guard is down.

These strategies proving ineffective, hand-to-hand combat begins: a swipe, a pinch, and for the smaller ones, a well-placed bite or two.

How do they learn the ways of war when we've tried to model the ways of peace? There are no guns in the house—real or make-believe. Only rarely are voices and hands raised in anger. Somehow this primitive lashing out must be rooted deep in the human psyche.

Sure, I could blame it on television, and I do to some extent. But I must look more deeply into my own behavior and words. Somehow I must be giving a double-message. I talk of peace, but do my sharp words occasionally belie my principles? Am I inconsistent in cutting off conflict when it begins? Or, in small doses, should I let their conflicts continue so they can learn to negotiate and compromise without violence?

There's no easy answer, as there was none for my parents when they would try to deal with sibling squabbles. More and more I find myself sounding like my own mother, though, when I echo her answer to "What do you want for your birthday, Mom?"

"Please, just one day without fighting."

&❧ TODAY: When my children fight I will not add to the fray by losing my temper. I will work with them to find a solution to their conflict on their own level.

Stinging Words

Set a guard over my mouth, O Lord;
keep watch over the door of my lips.—Psalm 141:3

AN EARLY MORNING RUN to the basement to throw in a batch of laundry so there'll be clean clothes for my child to wear in the school spring concert. My hand swoops down to grab a load of socks and jerks back as pain stings my hand then rushes up my arm. My immediate reaction: I've been bitten by a scorpion; this may be my final batch of laundry. Seconds later as my head clears and I calculate the likelihood of scorpions living in Ohio and in my laundry basket, I discover the source of my pain: a small bee nesting on the top of the pile. A vengeful stroke of a slipper puts an end to him and I make my way to the kitchen in search of ice to ease the pain. I remember the pesky bee buzzing around the laundry room light and the mental note I'd made to kill it when it landed—to spare my children a sting. Now I'm the one suffering as a result of my forgetfulness.

After treatment with ice, baking soda and ammonia (the only home remedies my friend and I can quickly recall), the localized swelling and dull ache remind me of the hours-old sting. As irrational as it seems, I know for a while I'll be careful to look before I plunge my hands into unknown piles.

This sting will heal. Not so the sting of words, I realize, as I ponder a biting verbal battle with my pre-teen daughter the previous day. "Like mother, like daughter," we attack with words rather than physical blows, each of us choosing the most apt, the most barbed comebacks to keep the argument from dying. (Over what now, I don't remember, the quarrels occur so frequently of late.)

In some ways the more mature, she calls a truce by bedtime, leaving a note on the kitchen table: "Mom, please don't go to bed mad at me. One of us might not be here in the morning." A little dramatic, but the right spirit. By bedtime, having kissed and made up, I nurse the wounds of her words even into the night; I hope she's resilient enough to slough off mine so she can sleep in peace.

With coworkers, and even in brief encounters with store clerks, I choose carefully the words I use. Why not with my children? My swollen hand is a well-timed reminder to me to speak as gently to them: The sting of the bee is a mere irritation next to the poison of my sharp words.

❧ TODAY: I will guard my tongue when I am tempted to lash out verbally at people, especially those I love.

The 'Sacrament' of Touch

Jesus on the breast of Mary feeding on her milk.
How long she must have delayed the weaning of such a
child!—Elizabeth Ann Seton

TO BE IN TOUCH with my children—infant, toddler, teen—what a gift. During those long nights of rocking and walking through colic or new teeth, I can easily forget that the wailing body I hold is a precious human life that needs touch to thrive.

My day is shaped by the "sacrament" of touch. In the morning, a kiss on the forehead to rouse my children, then another kiss when they resist the new day. A hug at breakfast as they groan about the early hour. More hugs as they race out the door, the yellow bus already rounding the corner at the end of the street.

At work, I miss those hugs, that special way of touching. Children are innocent enough to cry, "Mom, I really need a hug!" But most adults are hands-off lest we cross the lines of propriety. We are a touch-deprived culture, perhaps "bad touch" in some of our childhoods tainting our adult lives. Or maybe some of us are just cultural hybrids—one side of the family tactile, the other hands-off—unsure where touch fits appropriately in our own relations. I look forward to those after-work kisses, even half-hearted ones, to pump me up after a hugless day.

Nighttime, despite the struggle of keeping to a bedtime schedule, allows more privileged touch. Ritual backrubs, which I resisted for so long as too time-consuming, now are a finale to the day, a coming to peace and settling down for wornout children and parents.

"Stay just one more minute, please, Mom!"; I do.

"Come back, promise!"; I do, to find them nestled under covers, waiting for one last pat, a gentle peck on the head—the coda to my "touching" day.

🙞 TODAY: I will find an opportunity to surprise my child with an unsolicited hug or kiss.

I'm Proud of You

I often boast about you; I have great pride in you;...
—2 Corinthians 7:4

I 'LL ADMIT IT: My children are better than anyone
else's. They babble more intelligently, climb jungle
gyms more agilely, read their solo lines in the school
pageant more expressively. After all, they are *my*
children.

Before becoming a parent, I often wondered at the
rapt attention parents paid to what impressed me then as
insignificant acts of childhood: straining on tiptoe to drop
a letter in a mail slot, drinking a soda without spilling it,
sounding out an unfamiliar word. "What a big boy you
are" or "You're such a smart little girl," these parents
always seemed to be cooing.

Now that I'm a mother, I see with new eyes, and can
boast even more eloquently about what I formerly
viewed as the rather mundane, undifferentiated
accomplishments of children. Simply put, this new
worldview boils down to parental pride. I admit to a
large dose of it coursing through my veins.

Sometimes, to be sure, I must come across as offensive
and obnoxious to those less immersed in my children
than I am. I try not to whip out the most recent school
photos at professional meetings when colleagues inquire
politely over hors d'oeuvres, "And how are the
children?" I reserve for grandparents, aunts, uncles and
lifelong friends (preferably godmothers) the progress one
child is making on a challenging piano piece. Only

particularly literary friends get the benefit of my line-by-line (glowing, of course) critique of my third-grader's poem that's sure to be anthologized next to Emily Dickinson's.

Having voiced on occasion the belief that "you never say anything good about me," my children probably would be shocked to realize the self-control I exercise as I refrain from making them the centerpiece of every conversation I initiate.

No, not everyone sees my children as I see them. Of course, my children do have faults, which all too often I feel compelled to point out to them when they're with me. But when they're not, colleagues, beware! I can feel those parental pride hormones about to kick in.

&. TODAY: I will make a point of sharing with my children the boasts I made about them to my friends.

Cries in the Night

And I came to you in weakness and in fear and in much trembling.—1 Corinthians 2:3

THE LAKE STRETCHES OUT before me, shimmering with the last traces of a summer's burning sunset. Ahead of us, a few seagulls scamper for food, then flee, their shrill calls piercing the quiet night. But, suddenly the romantic landscape of my dream explodes as the "cry of gulls" persists, though the birds have fled. I slowly shake myself from my sleep and tune in to the unromantic reality of my darkened bedroom. More piercing than a bird, it's the cry of my child calling me from bed.

Half-awake and irritated at the nighttime intrusion, I walk the halls, unable at first to pinpoint which room the cries come from. This time it's not the baby, but the older child, covers thrown back, eyes glazed with fear. Not fully awake, but in need of comfort.

"A bad dream?" I ask, wrapping the covers and my arms around her. She trembles, from the cold and from the fright. "Tell me about it," I urge, rocking as she sobs incoherently about a rhino and an ostrich trying to bite her. Easing her slowly back to sleep, I linger to rub her head and assure her that the real world is safer than her dreams.

I remember my own childhood nightmares and the accompanying terror. When I was very young, only my parents' warm bodies next to mine on my bed were comfort enough to allow me to venture back into sleep where the dream might reappear. Older, living alone, I'd awaken and console myself with psychological explanations for the awful scenarios of those dreams.

But in the quiet of the night, when dreams seem as natural and as possible as reality, reason does little to stave off the bogeys that threaten us, whether we're children or adults. So, I hug her one more time, brush back her hair and tuck the covers about her, hoping that my love will linger as a guardian against the uncontrollable and unexplainable threats that haunt her in her dreams.

੩ TODAY: I will give my children extra hugs at bedtime and tell them of my love, to bolster them against the scariness of the night.

Treasures Lost...and Found

Or what woman having ten silver coins, if she loses one
of them, does not light a lamp, sweep the house, and
search carefully until she finds it?—Luke 15:8

T'S THE PERFECT ENDING to a summer vacation at the
beach. Hand-in-hand with two children, I jump into
the waves of Lake Michigan, letting the waters,
almost too warm from the August sun, pound over us.
My toddlers, both awed and frightened, wrap tiny fingers
around mine for security. As the waves subside, we head
back to shore. Something—the mossy gravel on the lake's
bottom or a slight undertow—sucks the youngest under,
as she loses her grip. Instinctively, I grab for her suit, pull
her up and comfort her as I carry her shaken to shore.

Within minutes we're calm. Only then do I notice a
difference in my hand. It feels loose, unnaturally so. At
first I conclude that my finger feels strange unattached to
a dependent child. Then I examine the hand. What's
missing is the ring. Not any ring, but the "heirloom" ring,
or one that was destined to be such. Tiny and gold, the
most precious jewelry from my husband's childhood, a
First Communion gift, his initials barely legible on the
worn signet. Since my birthday when his parents had
retrieved it and cleaned it for me as a gift, the ring and I
had been inseparable.

Now it was gone, slipped off as she lost her footing in
the lake. The loss hits hard. The ring had a future: a gift
on some special occasion for my children and eventually
theirs. It would be our way of marking the continuity of

generations of Barkleys.

Frantic, I head back into the shallow water, sifting through the sand and pebbles, unwilling to concede the loss. Later, when the children are settled in for the night, I comb the shore with a flashlight, hoping to find my treasure washed up farther down the beach.

But in a moment of insight, I let go, realizing the futility of the search and imagining what might have happened when she slipped from my hand. A lost ring or a lost child—in such simple terms, the choice seems absurd. I turn my back on the lake, and the ring, and hurry to embrace the true treasures in my life.

❧ TODAY: When my child loses or breaks one of my "treasures," I'll try to keep the loss in perspective, knowing how insignificant these material losses are in the larger scheme of life.

Telephone Ties

I think Mom was born to talk.—Annie Barkley, age 6

URING THE WORK WEEK, it's a menace, shrilly cornering me as I begin my day or reminding me of obligations unmet, calls not returned. Now it's everywhere, this nineteenth-century wonder turned twentieth-century nuisance. At one time, a link between distant offices or homes, a source of rescue in time of crisis. Now, an escape from person-to-person contact, so colleagues two doors away can expedite business without leaving their desks.

By workday, a technological burden. But on weekends the telephone is my ticket to escape and renewed friendship. This sometime-annoyance is transformed into a voice link with siblings, parents and friends—none within immediate reach without it.

On a Saturday morning, a close friend calls early, already in from a wintry jog with her dog. "I hope I didn't waken you!" "With children? Don't be silly," I reply. Her "quick call" to confirm details of the next day's dinner begins to escalate. First, we catch up on her outing with my child, her godchild, the weekend before. How can I refuse to let her brag about my daughter's beauty, her quickness of mind, her resemblance to me? Then, a brief update on mutual friends, their children, their problems.

My children, by this time having had their fill of Saturday cartoons, flash creative S.O.S.'s to me from across the room. The older ones resort to notes, shoving them between me and the phone. If they're really hungry, they'll use their own resources, I reason, as I settle into this delicious conversation. Now, the once burdensome phone becomes my escape—literally, as I pick up the portable version, extend the antenna and perch on the living room couch. Hot coffee in hand, I dive more deeply into the phone call, oblivious of the passing time.

"10:15! No wonder you're hungry," I apologize to my children as I hang up the phone. Deviant, I have neglected them for my own needs, for a refreshing half-hour conversation with a dear friend.

"You're going to see her tomorrow. What will you have to talk about?" my husband chides without malice, and perhaps with some envy. Maybe it's a "woman thing" or a "Mom thing." But every once in a while, a leisurely phone call, with no real motive, is just the right thing to lift my spirits after a wearying week of work.

❦ TODAY: I will call a friend or relative I don't talk to often and catch up on the trivial and significant details of our lives.

Thank-You's

And let the peace of Christ rule in your hearts, to which indeed you were called in the one body. And be thankful.—Colossians 3:15

TO GIVE WITHOUT COUNTING the cost, to serve without seeking rewards—they're ideals I strive for. But, c'mon, I'm human: I thrive on acknowledgment of my gifts shared. I don't ask for much, but a little gratitude goes a long way.

After a school program, I join other volunteers for applause from students and teachers, for a "thank-you" name tag shaped like an apple, for social time over coffee. As I scan the chattering groups, I feel almost embarrassed at being there: The steadfast mothers, volunteers with a capital V, dominate the room with their presence. No matter, my contributions, squeezed in on weekends and evenings, count too. Together we've shared the load; together we'll accept the thanks.

Other gratitude, not so public, perks me up even more: a thank-you card for volunteer service on a local board, a handwritten note from a busy friend grateful that I've helped her in a pinch, a note from a boss congratulating me on a project well-done.

But among my favorite thank-you's are the ones from my children—not prompted by any sense of political correctness or standards of courtesy, but bubbling out of a loving, grateful heart: A spontaneous hug accompanying the surprised "You made my bed today? Why? Gee, thanks, Mom." A note on recycled paper in the shape of a heart in primary print letters, "I love you. Thanks for being my mom." A hurried kiss on the way to the bus, "Thanks for typing that, Mom. I would've been up all night."

I need to be thanked, affirmed to recharge my self-image as a giving human being, to remind myself that those extras really aren't "extra" but essential to the smooth functioning of family, work, community. I can only give, give, give for so long without a little thanks, thanks, thanks. I'm sure it's not just my need, though probably few are as blatant in admitting it. In some well-documented psychological hierarchy, "the need for affirmation" must rank near the top for human beings of all ages. In seeking to fulfill my own needs, I sometimes lose sight of my children's. I can do for them what others do for me: let them know, unequivocally, how grateful I am for all they are in my life.

❧ TODAY: I will be sure to thank each of my children for one specific way they've made my life richer.

Workers' Compensation

*Dare Mom and Dad. I hoop you have a good day at wrok
Mom and Dad. I love you Mommy and Daddy. From
Annie.—Annie Barkley, age 6*

N O RAISES THIS WEEK. No stunning annual
performance reviews from the boss. But the
message painstakingly printed on my
daughter's chalkboard is reward enough. She beams as I
read it, proud of having thought of the message and of
her homemade spelling, corrected and re-corrected to
make the words just right.

I'm not sure she really comprehends what a "day at
wrok" means, but she has some notion. While she's at
school, I'm at work—the beginning of the parallels. There
are more. While she's printing letters on primary lined
paper, I'm typing memos on a computer. While she's
reading primers, I'm reading reports. She's out at recess,
I'm chatting with a friend over coffee. She scurries to
pack homework in her schoolbag, and I stuff papers into
a briefcase for some late night reading.

So often children think their lives and ours are worlds
apart, but there are more links than they imagine. As they
grow into each new phase of their lives, we wonder how
they will adjust. Will they be able to sit still in preschool?
Will first grade be too hard? How will they handle the
change of classes middle school brings? Before long,
they'll be out the door and living on their own in a
campus dorm.

Through each stage run connective threads: hard

work, enthusiasm for the task at hand, flexibility, cooperation, a sense of humor to allow them to laugh at their mistakes. These habits, learned young, will serve them well as they shed the worlds of childhood for the pursuits of mature living.

True enough, but the formula reads like a prescription for life penned by the granddaddy of all American work ethicists, Ben Franklin. Something's missing from this recipe for career success: the motivation. What spurs me on is more basic, an ingredient crystallized in the chalk wisdom of a six-year-old: a child's love that awaits me and assures me that no matter what my day at "wrok" has been like, my life has been a true "success."

🍃 TODAY: When I feel less than productive or successful at work today, I will call to mind the love my children hold for me.

The Joy of Pets

*And God said, "Let the earth bring forth living
creatures of every kind: cattle and creeping things and
wild animals of the earth of every kind." ...And God saw
that it was good.—Genesis 1:24-25*

"**Y**OU'RE CRAZY," I overhear one friend saying to
another about the purchase of a pet for her
family. "They're as much trouble as another
kid." In some ways, I'd have to agree.

Who needs the extra expense of dog food, cat litter,
gerbil bedding or costly visits to the vet for shots,
checkups and medications? Who needs the hassle of
changing the goldfish's water every other day (despite
the promise on the box of the desktop tank that the filter
will keep the water clean for weeks)? Who needs the
trauma of nighttime searches for gerbils who've escaped
from the cage sometime during the day? (Will we find it
alive? Or will the dog have sniffed it out first?) Who
needs messes on the carpet, scratches on the furniture,
pet hair on countertops?

We do. Because such annoyances quickly fade next to
the joys a pet brings to the family. The joy of the first fish,
scrutinized for hours by a toddler in awe of its fins and
bubbles. The joy of choosing a name, no matter how silly
it sounds to adult ears: PeeWee, Minnie, Lady or Inky.
The special pride of sharing a pet at preschool show-and-
tell and announcing, "He's my very own," and "Yes, you
can hold him if you're really careful."

And with these joys come lessons in caring, lessons

many adults have never learned, about being responsible for another living creature. Think twice when you leave the yard—if you don't close the gate, the dog may wander off. The gerbil cage smells really bad—how long has it been since you changed the bedding? Why is the dog drinking out of the toilet bowl? Did you forget to give her water this morning?

Along with chores, come love and friendship, not quite human love, but perhaps more tangible to a child. To sit lazily rubbing a pet's back and receive a purr or a grateful glance in return, without either child or pet asking more; to come to value the sacredness of life other than human—those are the intangible and lasting gifts our pets grace us with when we make room for them in our lives.

❧ TODAY: I'll spend some special time with my children and their pet—a walk, a few minutes of grooming, or a session in front of the fish tank to marvel at God's goodness in creating these animals for our delight.

Getting to Know You

Arise, my love, my fair one,
and come away;
for now the winter is past,
the ruin is over and gone.—*Song of Solomon 2:10-11*

WHO IS THIS MAN sitting at the far end of our kitchen table, cutting meat into childsize bites, wiping catsup from the corner of little mouths, correcting table manners? Basics, I still remember: his birthdate, our wedding anniversary, the color of his eyes (though it's been too long since I've gazed romantically into them).

The oft-quoted "children bring you closer together" is part fiction and part wisdom. Together we've rejoiced in the newness of their lives, shared the pain of accidents and illness, taken pride in all they've achieved. But our children wedge themselves between us too, calling us out of bed at night, interrupting conversations serious or playful, shaping our entertainment to their level of enjoyment.

We need to step away, to rediscover one another, because in the blink of an eye, our home, now straining at the seams with kids and toys, will be that proverbial empty nest. What will we talk of when there are no report cards to assess, Little League schedules to arrange, birthday parties to plan, sibling rivalries to arbitrate?

What did we talk of before their births? The comings and goings of friends and colleagues, tensions at work, career and life goals (starting a family!), favorite books and films, where to go on the next vacation.

So we dig into our pockets, assessing whether we can really afford the cost of a nighttime sitter, two movie tickets, a meal afterward. No, let's be less ambitious: a sitter and dinner for two. We'll ignore the whines of "But I can't go to sleep if you're not home!" and "We never get to go anywhere with you," kiss them good-night, and slip out, for just a few hours, into a world without children: where we talk in complete sentences with no interruptions; where we, and only we, eat off our own plates; where we sip a glass of wine without picking out bits of crayons; where we rediscover why we fell in love enough to want these precious children who are now the center of our lives.

❧ TODAY: I will plan a special time with my spouse—a breakast, a movie, an overnight—even if it means fudging a bit on the budget.

Old Friends

Friendship needs no words—it is solitude delivered from the anguish of loneliness.—Dag Hammarskjöld, Markings

THEY ENDURE—the real friendships rooted so deep that separations of months or years mean merely a pause, not a break in the bond.

Once, during the intensity of "courtship," I let my female friendships lapse, throwing all my energy into the new male-female relationship I was discovering; then no other friendships could compete. My true friends understood my need to bond exclusively during that romance-turned-to-love. And when I finally integrated this man-friendship into my life, they were still there, willing to continue, to integrate my new love into our old friendship.

Then through the all-absorbing stages of pregnancy, these friends persisted. Single themselves, they shared the anticipation, the details of birth, as if my children were their own—no jealousy, no admonitions to talk about something besides babies, only pure joy at my joy in the wonder of birth.

Too rarely now, we take time to be together, just two of us alone for dinner, a walk, a late-night drink. But when we do, I rediscover why we were drawn to one another years ago. There's an easiness here, an openness, permission to be who I am—mother, wife, daughter, career woman—but mostly just me, a friend. Comfortable together, we can tramp silently over a snow-covered mountain path or drive hundreds of miles with only an occasional comment. We signal with our eyes as we simultaneously notice absurd behavior, aware that if we hold our gaze too long, we'll explode in laughter. Which we do, once we're alone again to relive the moment.

In our conversations, the past is always present, but not dominant. We know what we've shared lays a foundation, but we've allowed one another to move beyond that base, to change and to grow in ways we might never have predicted years earlier when we first tentatively forged what's now an essential link.

Other friends from my past are only fuzzy memories— pictures in albums, topics of discussion at reunions, scrawled lines on yearly Christmas cards. But a few special women remain a constant in my life, reminding me of who I was in the past and challenging me to be real as we move on paths sometimes parallel, sometimes divergent, into our futures.

❧ TODAY: I will find a special card to send to my old friend to remind her how precious her enduring friendship has been in my life.

Vive la Difference!

If the whole body were an eye, where would the hearing be? If the whole body were hearing, where would the sense of smell be?—1 Corinthians 12:17

"I'M SEEING THREE OF THEM at school now—and get the feeling they're triplets"—this time from a teacher, but it's becoming a familiar refrain. I can't see the similarities, though I know there must be some strong family traits to elicit so many comments—their blue eyes, their infectious smiles, their energy and determination. But clones they're not.

Just when I think I can predict, on the basis of our brief family history, how one will act at the next stage of growth, they fool me, resisting easy and deadening classification. I know I must let them be different so that each be special.

One is meticulous and thoughtful, but in my impatience I label her slow—and deprive her of the gift, that if nourished, will shape her into her future self: an artist, a scientist, a patient parent. What are my criteria for "fast" and "slow" anyway, I wonder. My own harried life? A sibling who zips through tasks with ease, cutting corners, but looking perfect because of native ability?

One's a soccer star, aggressively circling opponents to whisk away the ball, then speeding down the field to assist in a goal. The other shows no interest in sports, preferring to lie in the shade near the hot field, scribbling temporary works of art in the dirt.

One's the star reader of her class, confident at the

microphone or on stage, basking in public attention. The other, no less talented, curls up in an afghan on a cool autumn day to finish the book begun that morning.

Leafing through family picture albums, I'm startled into admitting I can't identify which child I'm seeing without consulting the backs of photos to jog my memory. Maybe there are more physical similarities than I'm willing to admit to others who ooh at the striking family resemblance. Each is different, but I need to guard against ranking the differences as better or worse, as they continue to grow into those special, and very different, children who surprise even their own mother with their specialness.

&. TODAY: I will name something special about each child, telling them individually what gifts I value in them.

Looking Like a Mom

*For no one ever hates his own body, but he nourishes
and tenderly cares for it,...—Ephesians 5:29*

MY BODY IS A MOTHER'S BODY. There, I've said it
aloud, a good strategy to help me accept the
reality I still resist. Coming to terms with my
"new" body hasn't been easy. It's not just age. Women
older than I still possess the bodies of their youth. And
it's not related solely to weight gain or loss; at my
heaviest, most people consider me petite.

Still, my body after motherhood is a brand new one
that takes a little getting used to. Pregnancy has been one
of the culprits in this subtle transformation. Stretched
beyond the outermost definitions of elasticity (by a
growing fetus and a growing appetite unchecked by the
confines of everyday clothes), my old body never quite
made it back from that first nine months' out-of-control
journey. Naively, I didn't believe experienced friends
who'd warned me to kiss my prematernal image good-
bye. I was smug: All they lacked was a little willpower
and exercise. But reality and tears struck the first time I
struggled into my favorite pair of pre-baby jeans and
couldn't even begin to zipper them. Eventually, I did
shed the "baby weight" as I'd promised myself, but, as
my friends had promised me, the weight had all shifted,
foiling my efforts to return to the clothes of the past.

In part, this new "mother's body" has to do with
ownership. On elevators, in grocery lines during my
pregnancies, strangers felt free to pat my burgeoning

belly while asking such intimate questions as "Had much trouble with hemorrhoids yet?" or, with my two girls listening, "Are you trying for your boy?" Being part of the public domain annoyed me then, but I've since grown used to sharing my body with others, my children—first through months of nursing, then as an object of anatomical interest and amusement as they explore my hair, my fingers, the mole on my cheek and other body parts I'd hoped to have hidden from the congregation of the 9:30 a.m. Sunday Mass.

The changed look and the "Mom's body is mine" attitude are the down side of having this mother-body. But there's an up side, too. Without it, I would never have experienced the contented sucking of a nursing baby at my mother-breast, the swaying of a fussy toddler who can find comfort perched only on my mother-hip, the rhythmic patting of my child's hand on my back as she soothes herself to sleep on my mother-shoulder. Such joys only a mother's body can know. My new "mother body"—I've earned it, I'm proud of it. I think I'll keep it.

à TODAY: As I undress for bed tonight, I will offer a prayer of gratitude for all the mother-experiences that have shaped my present mother-body.

Elder-love

The institution is committed to respect for human rights and the sacredness and dignity of life at all stages.—Sisters of Charity Document on Sponsorship

W E ARE A NATION OF BABY-LOVERS, child-worshippers. We are obsessed with new life. Prenatal clinics, birthing classes, laws mandating infant car seats—all reflect the premium we place on life in its beginnings. We desperately want children, and we want them healthy and safe.

It's right that we should celebrate and cherish life so new and so fresh. Somehow, though, our interest wanes long before this deeply longed-for human life ends. Robbed of the strength that is the "glory of their youth," the elderly are relegated to the status of nonperson in the eyes of many. Many years earlier, a precious being whose every gurgle and movement was greeted with fanfares, the older person often slips anonymously and quietly from life, with no applause and little recognition of the value of many years.

Except for their own aging relatives, my children know very few older people. Elderly strangers in malls and on buses appear frightening—hobbling and slow, they are often an obstacle to youthful energy.

My children are too young to see beyond the externals now, but I hope as they mature they'll understand what rich lives those gray hairs testify to, lives marked

• by struggles through recessions and depressions, with incredible feet-first landings and a readiness to pick up and start from scratch;

- by promises made, vows kept, despite obstacles those of my generation could never fathom;

- by dreams achieved and dreams crushed, but spirits still intact and capable of dreaming;

- by sorrows beyond comprehension, tucked away in hearts that won't forget—giving birth to children whom they bury long before they themselves die;

- by wisdom earned not through books but through experience, wisdom rarely tapped by a culture in love with credentials and degrees;

- by peace beyond comprehension, rooted in knowledge and love of God, a peace fashioned by turmoil and pain, a peace this world cannot give.

&❥ TODAY: I will help my children act courteously to elderly people we meet, reminding them of the experience and wisdom inside those they often see merely as aging bodies.

Missing You

I missed you today at school, Mom...and my blankie too.—Annie Barkley, age 6

M Y CHILDREN HAVE this skewed notion of reality: They think missing is a "kid" thing. Maybe this distortion is partially my fault. Maybe it's because I don't often share how much they mean to me, how much I ache for them when we're apart. Too often I expect them to give the first hugs, to announce as soon as they walk in the door that they're glad to be home, that they missed me.

I need to learn to give the first hug with "I need a hug—I missed you so much today."

I need to share what I feel and think when they're gone:

- I begin missing you the moment you walk out the door, as I relinquish you to a world that's not always loving and nurturing. Standing at the bus stop, you're so little, yet so grown up. I miss the baby that you were.

- I miss you as I drive to work, scanning radio channels, then locking in on the station I always complain about listening to when you're along. I think I hear you in the back seat urging, "Turn it up just a little, Mom, that's my favorite song." I sing along and think of you.

- I miss you at lunch as I glance jealously at other mothers with their children: infants babbling in strollers, toddlers delighting in the mess of applesauce they've smeared on themselves and the highchair, teens in earnest conversation, oblivious to everyone nearby.

- I miss you and wish I could be with you more.

I don't have a blankie, but that doesn't mean I don't need one...or a well-worn bunny or a seasoned thumb. Even as an adult, I need something familiar and secure, a symbol to remind me of the comforts that await me at home—a warm bed, a crackling fire, a firm hug and sloppy kiss from the children I will always miss.

❧ TODAY: I'll lie in ambush for my children and be the first to attack with hugs and a sincere "I really missed you today."

So Beautiful

Ah, you are beautiful, my love;
ah, you are beautiful;....—Song of Solomon 1:15

"DO YOU THINK I'M PRETTY, Mom?" my oldest child asks in a moment of self-assessment before the mirror. "Don't say 'yes' just because you're my mother."

"You're beautiful," I reply in truth. But don't ask me to look at you out of anything but the eyes of a mother. No matter how you look to anyone else, you're always beautiful to me.

You're beautiful to me in your birth. The nurses may see a blood-covered, wrinkled, skinny-legged conehead, but to me you're spotless and fair—my miracle.

You're beautiful to me drooping in your high chair as you fight off your inevitable nap, mouth smeared with strained peaches, matted hair resting on hands clenched around a soggy biscuit. You're messy, but you're mine.

You're beautiful to me on lake-soaked beaches as you dig deeper into watery holes, sand in your hair, in your diaper, under your tiny nails. A horror to passersby, but to me you're a flawless sculpture in sand.

You're beautiful to me as you run injured down the street to my arms—your face, your elbows, your knees scraped and bloody. As I wash away the dirt, I feel the softness of your skin and know your scars and your scabs will be beautiful too.

You're beautiful to me as you confront me with my injustice, eyes burning (my own reflected in yours as you accuse me). Your anger isn't easy to bear, but your words shimmer with beauty because they're yours.

You're beautiful to me as you play and dance, at first awkward when you hop in time with a nursery rhyme, then, as you grow, fine-tuned in a graceful arch, a flawless catch in the outfield, an unexpected cartwheel on the lawn.

You're beautiful to me now as you question your beauty, hoping to find favor in others' eyes as your beauty shifts from a child's to a woman's, knowing even in your youth that mothers can see only beauty.

Ask me again, in two weeks or two years or two decades, and the answer will be the same and still the truth: "You are beautiful, my love, ah you are beautiful."

&❧ TODAY: I will tell my children how handsome or pretty they are, or compliment them on a physical feature that they might not appreciate.

Faith of Our Mothers

I am reminded of your sincere faith, a faith that lived first in your grandmother Eunice and now, I am sure, lives in you.—2 Timothy 1:5

"**M**Y WORST FEAR IS COMING TRUE—I'm becoming my mother." That's the gist of a playful caption on a friend's coffee mug. More and more lately I remind myself of my mother, but this realization brings no feelings of dread

Our genetic links are beyond doubt—the same nose (mine once cute and "pug" now bears more of a resemblance to her less flattering "bulbous nose"), the aging hair ("greyish brown" or "brownish grey," depending on who's describing it), the body of sturdy stock ("perfect for childbearing," someone once remarked; I took it as a compliment). My only regret is that in addition to her physical traits, the faith of my mother couldn't also be transmitted to me, some specific chromosome guaranteeing that I'd be the woman of God that she is.

Hers is a private faith, not a showy display of religiosity. As in all that she does, she lives out her faith in an understated way. Her faith is simple, innocent, straight out of the gospels. She's the living version of the works of mercy—visiting the sick, bringing food to the hungry, clothing the naked, instructing the ignorant, praying for the living and the dead—not for her own aggrandizement but for the sake of the Kingdom.

As schoolchildren we were urged to dedicate all our written work to God. On the righthand corner of our papers we'd neatly print the letters J.M.J. (Jesus, Mary and Joseph) or A.M.D.G. (for the greater glory of God). Those were routine gestures, often empty of meaning or motivation, but my mother's life is one ceaseless A.M.D.G. Now that her children are grown, she has the luxury of almost daily Mass. But even with small children, homebound to care for them, she prayed her way through the day, offering up disappointments and encouraging her children to do the same, reminding us that greater good would come of our temporary sadnesses, since not one sparrow fell to the ground without God's being mindful of it.

Today, as I watch my mother dedicating herself to her daily tasks at home—changing a grandchild's diaper, peeling vegetables for a family dinner, canning tomatoes from her garden—I hear her contentedly humming to herself (my father calls it "purring") and know that in her simple way she's at prayer. A woman happy and blessed and secure in her faith in the Lord, my mother makes her life a hymn of praise to her creator, her soul magnifying the Lord, her spirit always rejoicing in God her savior.

❧ TODAY: I will unite in prayer with the holy women, living and dead, who inspire me to spiritual growth by their quiet, vibrant faith.

Role Model

Hear, for I will speak noble things,
  and from my lips will come what is right;
for my mouth will utter truth;...—Proverbs 8:6-7

"I'D LIKE YOU TO MEET my mentor," my young friend announces with a proud smile to her out-of-town guest. The word "mentor" startles me; I glance around for a person to fit the title. No one here but me.

We have never defined our relationship that way, so the blatant statement catches me off guard. In an instant, I assume the role with the firm, self-confident handshake I think should characterize one with such an impressive title.

In my day, at her age, I never had a mentor, had known the word only from the pages of books. In retrospect, I assume my personal role model was my mother. And the nuns during twelve years of schooling must have inspired me professionally—what other women did I know with full-time careers? But who even dreamed of claiming a mentor?

Me, a mentor. The word slips so smoothly from her tongue, but catches on mine; it fits awkwardly, like new dress shoes still molding to the shape of my feet. The word is everywhere: in magazine articles, career pamphlets, titles of speeches. Certainly I've known my share of mentors who've been acknowledged publicly at awards ceremonies and acceptance speeches. Why am I so uncomfortable with the word?

It's the connotation, the image it carries that I'm not sure I'm ready to handle. Professionally, I'm glad to be a role model, as I strive for excellence in my career. But "mentor" suggests more, at least to me. She sees me as more than just a leader in my profession; to her I'm a "together" woman, able to integrate career, children, marriage. And I am, but the public results belie the private struggles: devoting enough time to work without depriving my children, pursuing my own learning while finding time to advance my children's, being an independent woman while still needing to be in relationship with the man I love.

I'm confident I'll grow into my new title, and some day cling to it like my favorite well-worn shoes. I'm flattered by her admiration and trust, but she must see me in the light of truth: not as a superwoman, but as a woman whose daily challenge goes beyond professional success to more personal values—happiness and wholeness.

ࢇ TODAY: I will nurture the professional and personal growth of young women with whom I work, careful not to be too much of a Pollyanna in my portrayal of the life of a professional woman with children.

Fallen Heroes

*The L*ORD *saw that the wickedness of humankind was*
great in the earth, and that every inclination of the
thoughts of their hearts was only evil continually. And
*the L*ORD *was sorry that he had made humankind on the*
earth, and it grieved him to his heart.—Genesis 6:5-6

IDEALISM AND HEROES—both privileges of the young.
"In the old days," as my children label my youth,
heroes abounded. Since I was a product of my time,
those I elevated to pedestals were most often men—
writers, saints, statesmen. I devoured the books of jungle
doctor Tom Dooley; listening to him in our small-town
high school auditorium was a starry-eyed teenager's
dream. Even though I was too young to cast a ballot, I
immersed myself in tales of politics and family life when
the young Catholic Kennedy took the spotlight; I was
mesmerized by his inaugural address and crushed at his
assassination. Later, my heroes turned from political to
spiritual, as I climbed "the seven storey mountain" with
Thomas Merton, adding book after book to my collection.

Now, again a product of my generation, I've grown
cynical of heroes. With each historical analysis and
journalistic investigation, I've become more wary of
singling out any human being for adulation. The dead
have been robbed of their virtues by disclosure of their
vices: One of my heroes has been revealed as a
"womanizer," another convicted of illegal financial deals
in robbing investors of life savings, still others (male and
female alike) of resorting to violence while proclaiming

peace. I blame no one, not "the media" or historians—I value the truth enough to concede my idols might have feet of clay.

Some bemoan the fact that today's children admire the wrong men and women: tennis players, baseball stars, singers and actors. True, their values seem askew, but in a world where every physical and spiritual wart comes under close scrutiny, maybe "heroes" have to be as ephemeral and transient as the world's shifting values. Then, when one sports hero goes down in defeat, when a rock singer's hits drop from the charts, disappointment is only temporary.

Perhaps heroes of superhuman stature are a relic of the past, when myth still held sway in our culture. Perhaps that's not all bad: The superheroes might be gone, but, idealist that I am, I bet if we keep our eyes open, we'll spot a few old-fashioned heroes right in our own neighborhood.

❧ TODAY: I will read or tell my children the story of one of my favorite Bible characters or saints, pointing out how his or her values are still lived out in the lives of people they know.

Teachers' Legacies

*Your word is a lamp to my feet
and a light to my path.—Psalm 119:105*

THEY'VE BECOME A PART of my personal history, though they've long ago drifted out of my life. Teachers for only a year or two, they never cease working their influence on my life. The gentle ones, the harsh ones, the jovial ones and the incompetent ones— each left a permanent mark on my impressionable mind.

I recall their faces as I mentally list their names, remembering nightmare assignments completed, class punishments meted out, odd mannerisms we ridiculed when their backs were turned. They remain who they were then to me, until I meet them again and release them from my child-fashioned molds.

A high school English teacher—the nun who terrorized us with her daily evaluations of our grammar, our clothes, our makeup—now looks fragile in her old age, but not much older than when I sat through class recitations of passages from *Macbeth*. Together we reminisce about our shared past—about literature, about writing, about the discipline she felt compelled to impose because "your parents sacrificed to give you a good education." Suddenly we're out of the past and focused on the present. She asks, How are your parents? How old are your children? Are they good students?

Now freed of the past, I can see her as she is: no longer gruff, but caring, and a woman of prayer. I comment on her medallion, the single piece of jewelry she wears, in stark contrast to her white habit. She smiles: "A gift from my nephew. He never forgets the anniversary of my entrance to religious life." For the first time, I'm allowed to glimpse a side of a teacher who until now had never been a real person: Even old teachers have human needs.

As we part, no hugs—that's too artificial for the distance still between us. Only a pledge from her of prayers for a morning's project I dread. As a cocky teen, I thought I'd grown beyond her in knowledge. Perhaps by now I have. But I realize it will be a long time before I catch up with her in my pursuit of wisdom and holiness.

📧 TODAY: When my children complain about their teachers, I will try to help them understand the gifts teachers share that they might not appreciate until they grow older.

Transported by Books

There is no frigate like a book
To take us lands away.
—Emily Dickinson, *"There Is No Frigate"*

O NCE UPON A TIME, there was a fair young maiden, who in her leisure would turn to a good novel for pleasure. She traveled to distant lands, rubbed shoulders with heroes and heroines, walked side by side with clever detectives as they unraveled mind-baffling mysteries. Book in hand, she was always happy.

But soon the fair maiden was no longer young or alone, although she was still happy. Coos and cries replaced the silence of her former life. Her adventure books stood on their shelves unopened, replaced by those she now deemed more useful: home health books, nursery rhymes, tales of cats in hats and little engines that could. New books in hand, she was still happy, but secretly she pined for a book all her own, as in the days of old.

Then one day arrived a gift from a friend, another onetime fair maiden, who, for the moment, had had her fill of books about children and for children. Seduced from her perfect parenting ways, this fair friend had tasted of the delights of her past life; brought up to be gracious and generous, she shared her treasure.

For days the gift lay examined but unread because the fair mother worried that she would slip into her old ways, becoming so enchanted by the book that she would forsake her motherly duties. So the fair mother stood firm.

Little by little, though, she felt herself weakening. The beautiful book called to her when she passed it each day, as she changed diapers, fixed meals, tended to homework, soothed bumps and scrapes. One night, however, the little book seemed to cast a spell over all who lived in the fair mother's house. The children, normally restless and needy at night, fell to sleep without fuss. And for a few hours silence reigned over their home.

It was only then that the fair mother realized this book from her friend was no ordinary book, but an enchanted gift sent from heaven. Without doubt I am blessed, she told herself. Throwing off her former guilt, she picked up the book, nestled in a chair and gave in to the charms of that special book that had so quietly and patiently waited for just the right time to rescue her from the everydayness of her new life and to transport her, for a few hours only, to worlds long hidden, but never forgotten.

❧ TODAY: I will visit a library or bookstore and find a "frivolous" book to read, even if it's only a chapter a night.

'Disabled' Children

From that moment on, he set himself to do everything
with twice as much enthusiasm. And where the arm had
been torn away a wing grew.—Nina Cassian, "A Man"

TO SOME, THEY'RE "disabled," but the label means little. They're able in body and probably more able in spirit than most children. It's the most obvious way to slot them, but it's the least essential.

No leg, a stub for a hand, eyes blinded at birth—heavy burdens for little children. As babies, they are protected from the gawks of rude bystanders by parents who cuddle and kiss them all the more to compensate for the insensitivity of strangers.

As they grow, in body and understanding, beginning to notice that they are different, sheltering does little for them and their self-esteem; now it is their burden. Return stare for stare? Flaunt the difference? Retreat into a sheltered world where the only adventures are inner? Whatever tactic works best, they must face the challenge head-on.

My own children, physically intact, try not to stare, but the young one is frightened. "Her mom took her leg home and she used crutches—it scared me, Mom." How to acknowledge the fear, valid in a six-year-old still wondering about the world and its inequities, while I crush any seeds of prejudice?

They're "disabled," but so "whole," able to look other children straight in the eyes and answer questions about life in a wheelchair (the only life they've known), share slightly off-color jokes in sign language, pass around their latest wig as they sprout a new crop of hair after cancer therapy.

They grow, not without pain and tears (and not without their parents' pain and tears), and so do their friends. True friends take the physical in stride and ignore the stares they too draw as companions of the "disabled." We who pride ourselves on being our children's teachers learn from them what really counts.

"You didn't tell me Jason was missing a hand!"

"What's the big deal, Mom? It's just a hand."

& TODAY: I will find a book to read to my children that will communicate on their level that physical "handicaps" should not be a barrier between them and other children.

The Gift of Teachers

Thank you for sharing your daughter with me. I am so blessed.—Ann Daugherty, teacher

OUR CHILDREN ARE "ours" for so little time. Omniscient and omnipotent for their early years, we parents relinquish those virtues once our children begin their formal education. Indeed, most days they spend more of their waking hours with their teachers than with us. Reflecting on this transfer of power, I'm awed: The parent-teacher relationship is a convenant, a sacred trust.

What do we risk sharing our children? They no longer see us as all-knowing. We abdicate our authority as the last word in correctness—in subject matter and manners—to virtual strangers. Even more frightening, for seven hours a day, our values move backstage to those of adults whose ethics are virtually unknown to us. What do they preach? What values do they live? Can we be sure we've found a match between theirs and ours?

What do our children gain through this shared risk? A broader view of life and learning, a growing sense of independence from adults called "parents," a move essential for children who soon will be autonomous persons. There's a deepening of self-worth when they're loved and respected by outsiders ("You're just saying that to make me feel good because you're my mom" replaced by "Mrs. X thinks I'm...").

But this moving out from the closeknit unit of the home benefits more than the children; as a parent I grow too. How am I doing? Are the values I've promoted ones that can survive outside the hothouse of the family? Have my prodding and nagging and affirming paid off? I send them off to the classroom, and then I wait. For feedback, positive or negative, to let me know how my children are doing. For a jolt of reality when they fail or succeed, to let me know how I'm doing.

Sometimes I don't want to hear what these "outsiders" have to say. Sometimes I resent the bonds growing between my child and a teacher who rates more esteem than I do.

But sometimes I'm affirmed in unexpected and surprising ways by teachers' assessment not only of my children but of my parenting: "I hope my child grows up to be like yours." "Can I take her home and keep her for a while?" "They're lucky to have parents like you." I savor these words, storing them away to be retrieved on those occasional dark days of parenthood when any glimmer of light is a treasure.

❧ TODAY: I will let my children know how much I value their teachers and their influence on our family, even though I don't always agree with their methods or policies.

Quiet Time

Creatures speak in sounds. The word of God is silence.
The secret word of God's love can be nothing but
silence. Christ is the silence of God.—Simone Weil,
"Random Thoughts on the Love of God"

AS THE CAR ODOMETER rolls over to 90,000 miles, one by one the amenities of what was once our "luxury" car begin to break down. First, the air conditioning. We can live without that for a few more weeks until the city summer descends with brutal force. Next the radio, skipping from station to station, unresponsive to our commands. Perplexed and annoyed, we adapt, reflexively punching in the stations we've temporarily lost. Then, catastrophe—all FM stations disappear. My oldest mourns the loss of her favorite songs. "You won't die," I assure her, but wonder how I'll start each day without my customary morning news programs.

The AM alternatives too chatty, I choose to switch off the meaningless noise. At first, the silence is discomforting. Too busy to read more than headlines in the morning paper, I've relied on the radio as both companion and informant on my long drives to work. Feeling deprived and cheated, I wonder how I'll hold my own in office conversation about world news.

Gradually, though, a few days into my deprivation, I begin to welcome these morning retreats. The whirring of cars next to me on the highway, the shrill sirens of ambulances down the road fade into background noise.

The quiet nurtures activity within. Conflicts with friends, decisions about staff, confusion over children's extracurricular schedules—formerly submerged, now rise to consciousness, where I confront them one by one. Often harried by loose ends from home and work, now I welcome this focusing time for sorting through concerns.

Some days, the problems minimal and easy to dispose of within a few miles, I turn more deeply inward, to a level of prayer. I remember those I've promised to pray for: a young woman soon to be confirmed, my friend's mother struggling with cancer, students worried about final exams. Prayers of petition exhausted, I open myself to others: thanksgiving for husband and children, praise for the passing dogwoods, redbuds and azaleas...and for a God who speaks in wordless ways through broken radios and unbroken silence.

❧ TODAY: I will turn off external noises that are under my control so I can get in touch with the quiet within.

The Wisdom of Age

Gray hair is a crown of glory;
it is gained in a righteous life.
—*Proverbs 16:31*

"WERE YOU ALIVE during the Civil War?" and similar questions from my children remind me that to the young, old age is relative...and sometimes scary. I tell them I'm not really old because I have children who keep me young. But, the truth, which they're too young to understand, is that I'm not serene and wise enough to be called "old."

"Old" is the 65-year-old mother of four and grandmother of many who tells stories of segregation and discrimination, who brings to life for me, with no hint of malice in her voice, a blot on her country's history. Together we worry over recent news reports of renewed prejudice, cross-burnings, racial slurs. "Oh, honey, there's nothing new under the sun," she reflects, repeating her favorite passage from Scripture. And, despite the pain of her memories, she's at peace with what has been and hopeful that today's "youngsters" will fare better.

"Old" is a 75-year-old Hispanic friend recalling the children she's taught over the long span of her classroom career. Her love of her native language spills out in her excitement over a well-crafted Spanish sentence; her love of life and learning thrills me as she recounts the difficulties she's facing mastering French, the fifth language she's adding to her repertoire.

"Old" is a 67-year-old friend and mentor, famed for her grace and beauty as a young woman, now even more beautiful in her age. Fighting a degenerative eye disease that could rob her of her sight and her job, she doesn't whine (few people even suspect her disability), but reaches out to others younger than she in the support group she leads for those likewise afflicted.

As a child, I feared old age, associating it with crotchety, wizened residents of stale-smelling nursing homes I visited while caroling at Christmastime; as an adult (not old but aging), I look forward to its pace and its peace. For now, though, I'm immersed in the world of the young. I have miles to go before my life will have been "righteous" enough to have earned me that "crown of glory."

&❧ TODAY: Out of respect for the wisdom of old age, I will go out of my way to talk to an older person, especially one who's been dismissed as senile or burdensome.

Send in the Sun

Light is sweet, and it is pleasant for the eyes to see the sun.—Ecclesiastes 11:7

OVERCAST AGAIN TODAY, the twentieth day without the comfort of the sun's rays. My inner doldrums mirror the weather; though I try not to be mastered by my environment, I sure could use some sun.

Always a failproof topic of casual conversation, the weather now becomes a central theme, edging out international conflict and local politics. At work, we pause mid-conversation to note a cameo appearance by our absentee sun before it disappears for who-knows-how-long.

Plants set in windowsills at home and in the office reflect my listlessness. Even my children, usually undaunted by snow or rain or sleet or hail, comment on the bleakness of the weather. "Go outside to play," I suggest on the weekend as the ruckus of horseplay rattles my nerves. "It's too cold," they reply, as they jump back into the fray.

But it's not the temperature that keeps them in. These are the same kids who don layers of shirts and socks and boots and gloves to shovel snow or ride bikes...in January. What they perceive as an excess of cold is, in reality, the absence of sunshine.

No wonder ancient peoples deified the sun—not just for its power to germinate seeds and hurry along the harvest, but for its power to heal the spirit. The Church, in tune with the rhythms of nature, echoes the image. "O Radiant Dawn, splendor of eternal light, sun of justice," begins one of the "O Antiphons" that express our Advent longing for the messiah. We, the people who have dwelt in darkness await a great light.

I try to rise above my soul-weariness that's reinforced by day after day of rain and gloom. I've taught my children that they can control their moods; I need to model that control.

As I wait for the sun to venture forth from behind layers of enemy clouds and reestablish permanent residence in our corner of the world, I take comfort in distant memories of radiant warmth. I'm trying to be patient, but I can't wait much longer; I sure could use some sun.

🦋 TODAY: To compensate for my sun-deprivation, I'll read and meditate on Jesus as the light of the world (John 1:1-18).

At Their Own Speed

They also serve who only stand and wait.—John Milton, "On His Blindness"

WHEN I SEE THEM RUNNING on the playground or the soccer field, I hesitate: Could these be my children? Such single-minded purpose, such incredible speed. No, these creatures move swiftly, while mine haven't quite internalized the meaning of the words "right now"...when it comes to meeting my deadlines.

"Just let me sleep five more minutes, Mom!"—as the clock eats up minutes until the school bus arrives.

Once-hot cereal thickens into cold slime on the kitchen counter as the youngest changes shoes...for the third time this morning. "They're not tight enough, Mom."

The local weather on the television signals half past the hour, time to start rounding up children. But where are they? Scattered around the house in bathrooms, basements and bedrooms ("Get up now!").

In grade school religion classes, I blithely rattled off lists of virtues we Christians should strive for: charity, joy, peace, patience.... Obviously the musings of a celibate who didn't have to deal with children each morning before work. Patience should have headed that list, the crowning virtue that would assure immediate entry into the Kingdom.

Patience means one more pat on the back for a three-year-old buttoning her own shirt...while my stomach churns with anxiety over the meeting I'm almost late for downtown.

Patience means sighing quietly instead of screaming with frustration as an eight-year-old takes out her braids (is this the third or fourth time?) because "they're too bumpy."

Patience means not tossing off a sarcastic remark to the teen who can't find a math paper after assuring me the night before, "Sure, Mom, I've got everything out for school."

God's ways are not my ways, says the Bible. And my children's pace is not mine. They move to a different beat. I can only wait patiently, knowing that all too soon they'll be leading the frenetic life of busy adults and I'll be slowing down, our roles reversed in a delicious twist of fate.

❧ TODAY: I will build a little extra time into the morning, even five minutes, so I don't have to nag my children (so often) about getting ready on time.

Over-scheduled

Save me, O God,
for the waters have come up to my neck.
I sink in deep mire,
  where there is no foothold.
—Psalm 69:1-2

THIS WILL NEVER WORK, I sigh, as I lay my personal calendar and the family calendar side by side for scrutiny: two ballgames (same child, same night, different fields), a scout event and a monthly commission meeting for me at church. One car plus two parents plus four different destinations—not a formula for a tranquil evening. A friend with four children faces a worse plight—practice for First Eucharist for one child, softball for another, an awards ceremony for yet another and her husband out of town.

We pray for rain.

By early afternoon, a thunderstorm soaks the ground; the raindance my friend has promised must be paying off. But soon the sun reemerges and the drying process begins. Nearby I hear telltale sounds of lawnmowers as neighbors tackle grass overdue for cutting. Though softball cancellations seem out of the picture, the promise of rainouts has made me desperate for a night off, for a leisurely family meal. No rain in sight, but weather conditions seem ripe for a spring tornado; for a few minutes I fantasize about a sudden "tornado watch" that would cancel the night's game. I return to reality, aware that such daydreams won't promote mental health and won't remedy my present calendar jam.

By dinner time, I'm resigned to another hectic night. Then the coach calls: The fields are still soggy, so all games are off. Her hopes buoyed by the sunshine and the promise of her first game, my nine-year-old collapses on the floor in tears, arguing that we could move the game to another town down the road where the fields might be drier. Outwardly I console, but inside I rejoice. One down.

On to the evening meeting, and catching a ride with a friend to free up the family car for small errands. "Can you bring me home if I can get a ride there?" I ask over the phone. A pause. "Wait a minute, is that tonight?" she wonders. My calendar says tonight, hers tomorrow, so I scurry from the phone to check the meeting agenda. She's right, I'm wrong. "Need a ride tomorrow?" she offers. I won't even think about what tomorrow's schedule might look like—probably impossible—but I'll worry about that tomorrow. Tonight I'm home free.

❧ TODAY: I'll clear the family calendar of inessentials even if the eventual result is a cluttered night down the road; I need a night at home.

Waiting Rooms

But if we hope for what we do not see, we wait for it with patience.—Romans 8:25

WAITING ROOMS—they're so well named. How many hours I've spent in them—early morning visits to the orthodontist, eye exams squeezed in before work and before school. These hours the waits are dreamy and easy, my hands curled around a carryout coffee, the chatter of morning radio news in the background as I skim through my appointment book to remind myself of what the day holds. Sleepy-eyed, even the children are subdued.

But most times, reality: wall-to-wall waiting jammed into the end of an already-hectic day. Moms and dads in business attire cradle flushed and droopy babies. And we wait, hoping that something's progressing behind the closed door which never seems to open to let us in or others out.

No room to roam, healthy toddlers in tow for another's appointment climb precariously on tipsy chairs, unmindful of parents' repeated pleas to "just sit down, it's almost our turn." Elbow to elbow already, we wonder who will shift positions to let another find a spot to sit and wait. A mother's loud sigh echoes the impatience we all feel...and the cumulative stress level seems to rise.

"Are we next?" my youngest whines, noting accurately that a child who arrived after us has been called before us. "Probably an emergency," I whisper without much conviction. I can offer no sound answers but can only counsel patience. Once I admit that my schedule has already been sabotaged, I settle in, grateful that the ringing phone won't be for me.

These moments of respite are a gift, I come to see, a blessing I could not have predicted. One child snoozes on my lap, the other nestles in the chair next to me. In our waiting, we're content just to spend some unexpected time together.

❧ TODAY: While waiting with my children for appointments, I'll spend that time really listening to and sharing with my children the events of their day.

Guardian Angels

For he will command his angels concerning you
to guard you in all your ways.
On their hands they will bear you up,
so that you will not dash your foot against a
stone.—Psalm 91:11-12

NGELS HAVE GOTTEN A COLD SHOULDER the
past few decades. In this age of more pressing
philosophical problems, who cares how many
of them can dance on the head of a pin? Does it really
matter if we distinguish cherubim from seraphim in the
heavenly pecking order? Still, Scripture assures us of
their protective presence. If that weren't evidence
enough, consider the recklessness of children.

Case in point. Your toddler wanders away from you
in a crowded shopping center, following skirt and shoes
she's sure are yours. Your panic is mirrored in your
husband's eyes and tone: "I thought she was with you!"
Minutes later, you scoop her up from her peaceful perch
near the mall's center fountain, unsure who to thank for
her rescue.

Next scenario. You've followed every safety
precaution in the parenting manual to childproof your
home, hiding the poisons behind locked doors, putting
hot pans (handles turned in) on back burners, installing
smoke alarms on every level of the house. What more can
you do?

"Be good while I take a quick shower," you warn your
five-year-old. Returning to the kitchen minutes later to

finish dinner, you find him munching the candy you'd squirreled away in the topmost cupboard. Impossible, you think, until you see the teetering tower of chairs and stools near the stove he's climbed on to retrieve his prize. Anger and relief for his safety mingle in your quick prayer of thanksgiving to whatever spirit protected him in your absence.

Moving into adulthood, I relegated the guardian angels of my childhood to the realm of the Easter Bunny and ghosts in the graveyard. But my children have restored my faith in angels' protective powers. Although I'm not as convinced as some that we all have our own personal angels sitting on our right shoulders, I know they're hovering nearby when they're needed most...because, God only knows, mothers can't be everywhere.

&ed; TODAY: Without lapsing in my care or attention to my children, I will thank God for the gentle guardianship of angels when a "near miss" might have turned into a disaster.

Sick Leave

Be gracious to me, O LORD, for I am languishing;
O LORD, heal me....—Psalm 6:2

ITH THE FIRST SYMPTOM—the unforgiving throbbing in my head—I resist the truth. Sure, I've seen my coworkers dropping daily around me, and my children have complained of sore throats, headaches, fevers, but I'm one of the untouchables, priding myself with my perfect attendance record. Me, sick? Out of the question. Besides, Moms never get sick.

So I forge on with all the optimism and willpower I can summon up, for two days forcing pills to relieve the ache of now more than just my head, but my whole body. I'll conquer it this weekend, I resolve. Between trips to the grocery and church I collapse in a chair or on the couch to block out the pain that stubbornly refuses to yield to my healing thoughts. Ever optimistic, on Sunday evening I review my Monday-morning schedule and lay out clothes in anticipation of the off-to-school-and-work morning whirlwind.

By morning, the whirlwind has been upgraded to a tornado, raging within my head. Disoriented and out of sync ("Toto, I don't think we're in Kansas anymore"), I muster up the energy to locate lunches, backpacks and coats, then collapse on the couch in an afghan cocoon.

I've never been so tired or in so much pain, I groan to no one but myself. Well, maybe during pregnancy and childbirth, but at least there was a reward for all the trouble. Alone, my now-healthy children all at school, I long for a mother to mother me, to rub my back, to tell me this pain won't last forever. It's the ultimate in regression, the classic wish to return to the womb ("There's no place like home, there's no place like home").

At the end of a restful day, I pull myself together for the return of my children, who, though sympathetic to my illness, will still demand from me affection, attention and motherly comportment. Moving out of illness toward healing, I reflect on my overly dramatic whining and death wishes. People live constantly in pain, and life goes on for them and those they love, I realize with embarrassment, grateful no one had tuned in my soap-opera thoughts. Always in control, often critical of those who aren't, I emerge from my brief illness a bit humbled and more sympathetic to my children's complaints of aches and pains and their need for extra cuddling to hurry them along to wellness.

❧ TODAY: When my children begin to show signs of illness, I will put aside less important chores to spend extra time holding and soothing them.

The Death of a Pet

Rejoice with those who rejoice, weep with those who weep.—Romans 12:15

I T'S THE FIRST IN A SERIES of pet deaths, none of them easy, each teaching something more about life's cycles and disappointments.

First, the goldfish, Bonnie. The first real pet our child ever had, won after countless trips to the goldfish booth at the parish carnival, worth spending tickets that could have gone to surer prizes. We might have bought a school of fish for the money squandered on the pet that all too soon floated dead in a bowl. Forty-eight hours—hardly long enough to bond in human terms, still a blow to a six-year-old who'd named and nurtured it these two days.

Then the gerbils—first Pee Wee, the favorite, of pneumonia. More painful than any fish death, since we watch her wasted body contort in pain until we finally laid her to rest in a backyard grave. Several gerbil funerals later and the older children have caught on to the rhythm of life and death, and the finality of burial. "Daisy won't be able to breathe down there," the youngest worries. "She's dead, she's never going to breathe again," the eight-year-old explains.

For these small, short-term pets, the grief lasts briefly. But with the family dog, it's different. Together we watch her grow old, lose sight, hearing, spend more time sleeping than romping. As her legs fail, we begin to warn that some day she too will have to die. Too soon, it seems, that day comes. Unlike a fish in a bowl or a gerbil in a cage, she was present everywhere: curled up next to us under an afghan on a couch, lying in the sun as the family raked leaves, annoying us as she dug in trash left uncovered or whined to be let outside.

So, another death the family must face. Each of us deals with the loss in our own way, but all of us grieve. To our petless friends, we're excessive and sentimental. But others, those who know the niche a pet fills in a family, understand the void this last death has left in our family's life.

❧ TODAY: I will remember the sadness I feel over our pet's death when I hear of pet deaths in the future, and I will take time to share kind words or a note consoling their owners.

Absentee Mom

My soul melts away for sorrow;
strengthen me according to your word.
—*Psalm 119:28*

L OUSY TIMING, I NOTE, as I read the list of special activities at school this week. A lunch with children smack dab on the day and at the time when I know I won't be able to get away from work. Other years, I've been able to juggle and rearrange to show up for most important events of the week, but this year it's not looking good.

My youngest doesn't take the news well. Bad enough that I had to miss the Thanksgiving feast last year at her kindergarten (a tragedy we salvaged by having her sit next to her best friend's grandmother), but the first parent lunch of the first grade—she's chagrined. "Mom," she says tearfully, "everybody else's mom will be there."

Of course, I know this isn't true, but what's important is not reality but her perception of reality. "What can I do?" I answer, her watery eyes riveted on me, hoping for some magical solution. "You know I have to work. I can get there the next day for the special Mass." It's not the same, she insists. I agree. In a moment of insight, we send off a homemade invitation to her grandparents, also invited for lunch. An hour and a half away, they'll come if weather and health permit. Maybe we're off the horns of this dilemma.

Even as I write a late-night note to accompany the invitation, I realize why the date nags at me: My parents have scheduled an out-of-town trip to be with my aunt following surgery. Disappointment will soon reign again in our home.

I love my work. I love sharing my aspirations and successes with my children, modeling for them that women can be good moms and good career women. What I don't love are days like this when even a somewhat flexible schedule doesn't mesh with my children's activities. I know it's not just a working-mom dilemma. Many fathers feel the same pulls, and many mothers at home full time can't always participate in school events because of other parenting demands.

The writer and the organizer in me loves stories that end with closure, especially a happy one. I suspect this is one chapter in our family's story that will never be written to anyone's full satisfaction.

&. TODAY: Though I can't make it to my child's special event, I will give an extra good-bye hug and assurance of my love before we part.

Money Woes

For the love of money is a root of all kinds of evil, and in their eagerness to be rich some have wandered away from the faith and pierced themselves with many pains.—1 Timothy 6:10

"BUT WHY CAN'T I BUY IT, Mom? It doesn't cost much."

I'm tired of half-truth responses, like "Just because you see it, doesn't mean you need it" and "It's not in the budget." So far, backing into the topic hasn't worked, so I tell them straight out: "Because we don't have the money."

I'm not asking to be rich—I've read all the warnings in Scripture—I just want to have to struggle less. The family budget we've so carefully crafted lies in shambles on the desk, a victim of unexpected minor and major bills. The gym shoes I thought would survive at least two months of nursery school come home ripped at the soles. Extra hours this week at work have hiked up child care costs. And the whole house seems to be caving in, room by room: a doorknob that no longer turns, a patch of water on a bedroom ceiling, a water heater strained beyond capacity.

"How dare you complain!" I challenge myself as I pass through neighborhoods where families are barely subsisting. Weathered faces peer emptily out of dirty windows held together with tape. Children too scantily dressed for the harsh winter hover around their defeated-looking mother as she emerges from a corner store with one bag of groceries. I feel foolish and selfish when I remember opening the most recent utility bill and grudgingly writing out a check as I vow to set the thermostat lower this winter. At least I have a working furnace and money to pay the bill, I remind myself.

Still, I chafe under the pressures. Financial stability isn't the measure of family happiness, but it is one thread in the fabric of family life, a thread that now seems stretched too tight, throwing the design out of kilter. Or could it be that I'm concentrating on the wrong design in the fabric? "My ways are not your ways," the Weaver gently reminds me in prayer as I reflect on the choices I have that the poor are denied. My economic "problems" are really just irritations, I begin to understand, ones that allow me to glimpse the inescapable burdens of the lives of those who peer desperately from behind frosted windows.

• TODAY: When I get depressed about how many things we can't afford, I'll make a mental list of all the material goods we take for granted that for others are luxuries.

Sleepless Nights

Oh sleep! it is a gentle thing,
Beloved from pole to pole!
To Mary Queen the praise be given!
She sent the gentle sleep from Heaven,
That slid into my soul.
—Samuel Taylor Coleridge, "Rime of the Ancient
Mariner"

I'M NOT PARTICULAR, I'll take it in any form for any reason—the flu, bronchitis, a broken leg, a blizzard. Just let me sleep!

How long before my coworkers notice that I'm not noticing...what they're saying, where I am, what I'm doing? So what can they expect of their zombie-friend? Perhaps I should have called in sick today and faked some illness. But, caught, how could I persuade a doctor to fudge a medical statement describing my "illness"—sleep deprivation?

Some day, when moms rule the world, we'll have sleep banks, like blood banks, to store up unused, unappreciated sleep from days before children. Those late Saturday mornings when I groused about the neighborhood children out early (10 a.m.!) pounding the pavement with basketballs and filling the morning air with exuberance—I'd gladly trade a few hours from each of those sleep-in weekends to add on at night or early morning now. A little comp time earned in my previous life.

Even to bed late and up early wouldn't be all that bad

with a decent night of sleep sandwiched between. It's the ups and downs of nighttime that drag me down. Up for the restless one still roaming the halls as I'm just getting cozy under the comforter. Then the midnight storm, its lightning and thunder rousing me as I lie on the edge of the bed, knowing what's next: "Mom, I'm scared!" Crisis handled, snuggled back in, on the verge of REM-sleep— the telltale thump of the youngest falling out of bed, then a wail.

By now, my internal clock tells me even without consulting the clock-radio that the end is near. One hour till rising. Should I try to sleep, knowing that the alarm will scream, just as I rediscover the best part of my oft-interrupted dream? What's that—part of my dream? A siren wailing? No, more like a dog wailing. So that's what I forgot the last trip up—the dog whining to come in from her nighttime trek to the backyard.

"Oh sleep! It is a gentle thing..."—a mother's pipe dreams.

&⦆ TODAY: When the children hit the bed tonight, so will I, no matter how many dirty clothes or unwashed dishes beckon me to stay up just a little bit longer.

Accepting Defeat

Let us not become conceited, competing against one another, envying one another.—Galatians 5:26

THEY HOLD HANDS AND CROSS THEIR FINGERS, smiling broadly in anticipation of winning. This is it—the awards ceremony for the all-day academic competition. I'm there to join in the celebration of their hoped-for success, a partner in the project for months: rounding up helpful resources for their research, arranging trips to the library and craft stores, giving honest feedback on posters, proofreading papers. Winners in the school competition, my daughter and her friend have advanced to the city finals. Now they eagerly await more ribbons to carry home.

As an outsider, more objective, I hold little hope of their being named among the top three. Here competition is stiffer, and from advance reports, the judges have criticized the project on points we've not anticipated. Still, the two beside me are confident.

The announcements begin in their division: first place, second place, third place—but no mention of their names. Graciously they applaud the winners, cheering loudly for an honored classmate. But through their brave smiles, tears of disappointment.

The drive home is sober as they dissect the judges' reports, savoring the praise and arguing against faults found. Not a judge or expert in the field, I try to remain neutral, though some of the criticism seems off-base, from adults expecting too much scholarship from mere children. True, more study, more care in the project might have paid off, but they had devoted weeks to preparation. They had presented their best.

How to wring a lesson from defeat, a scenario that would be repeated in varied forms throughout their lives: in athletic tournaments, at spelling bees, on college entrance exams, before personnel committees and final interviews with CEOs? "You did your best" and "Think how much you learned that you never knew before" are my feeble words of consolation. Then I keep still, listening to them as they work through defeat, voices brightening with comments like, "Now I know how the other kids must've felt when we won regionals and got to go to state." And, by the end of the ride, "We had a really good time with the other girls and guys from our school. It was a fun day."

By this point I am content with the one job only I can do well: chauffeur. My positions as counselor and philosopher have been relinquished to and more than adequately filled by the two twelve-year-olds chatting happily in the back seat.

ネ TODAY: When my children lose in competitions, I will comfort them, praise them for their efforts, then help them move beyond their disappointment.

Chronically Ill

Refrain from anger, and forsake wrath.
Do not fret—it leads only to evil.—Psalm 37:8

ONE YEAR SINCE HER LIFE has changed forever. A lingering illness, then the sudden and devastating diagnosis of a disease that will last a lifetime.

She remembers the date, the times, the events in precise detail—that day a touchstone for other events in this past year. "A year ago at this time we were in the emergency room. Remember, Mom?" Searching my memory, I resurrect details that I would prefer remain buried. But she won't allow it.

At the mention of the coming "anniversary," I suggest a family meal to mark the occasion. What will we name this meal? A celebration? Hardly. Yet it seems fitting that we gather to formally recognize the year that has ended. A quiet meal at her favorite restaurant. No toasts, no songs, no gifts at our table. The meal over, we gather belongings and return home to a routine that has been adjusted to fit a new definition of "normal." The meal may be over, but not the feelings it's revived in me: sadness and anger. For months after the diagnosis I was in a state of denial. I'd awaken some mornings thinking, "Soon it will pass, this temporary phase in our life." I'd scan the newspapers for medical reports hinting at breakthroughs, then remind myself to live in the present.

"Why did this have to happen to me?" she occasionally cries, and I'm glad resentment disrupts her seemingly mature adjustment to the changes in her life. "I can't answer that, but we'll make the best of it," I reply with an exterior calm I hope masks my inner anger.

Anger at whom, I wonder, as I find my body tensing and tears flooding my eyes in moments when I've let my emotional reserve slip. At fate, at researchers too slow to find cures, at the luck of the draw in genetic makeup...at God, I admit. God didn't cause this, I reason, but I need a scapegoat for displacing my anger. And surely God's big enough to handle that role. It feels good to be angry. Though it solves nothing and can't change reality, it serves its purpose: cleansing me of emotions that prevent me from seeing clearly. From seeing how fortunate we are that her disease is treatable, how we're blessed with nurses and doctors committed to her well-being and with friends who've integrated this new wrinkle into already solid bonds. And blessed most of all with a daughter who has inspired me to integrate my own anger into positive actions we can control, despite circumstances we can't.

❧ TODAY: When I feel my anger surfacing about my child's illness, I will perform a positive action that I know will benefit her health, so I will feel less out-of-control.

Unspeakable Loss

The LORD is near to the brokenhearted,
and saves the crushed in spirit.—Psalm 34:18

I N PASSING, over a quick breakfast of bagels and juice, the news doesn't register on my still-drowsy mind. I skim the headline and a few paragraphs, noting without feeling or interest that three youngsters have died in a gruesome auto accident in the early morning hours. Once at work, seeing the shocked faces of friends and hearing hushed communication of funeral details, the truth sinks in: That cold line of newspaper type translates into the death of a child of someone I know.

Death is never easy to speak of, to think of—because in allowing the reality into our consciousness, we allow for the reality in our own lives. And that means pain. We push it back, aware that some day we will lose a mother, a father, a spouse. But this death is too cruel—a child! No matter that he was already a young man; he was her child. She watched him grow out of diapers into toddler jeans and then soccer shorts; she watched him don graduation cap and gown and move into the adult world. He was her child.

How do I comfort these parents in their shock and grief? Remind them of their still-healthy, still-living children? Absurd. Preach about God's goodness and special love for their dead one? Sacrilege to parents with gaping holes in their hearts. Avoid the issue for a few months while they heal? The cowardly way...and they'll never really recover from this pain.

"I'll pray for you" sounds so feeble in the face of such profound pain, but that's the best I can do for now. "I'll pray for you" carefully and prayerfully written on a card they can cherish as each new stage of death confronts them—past the mind-numbing funeral Mass, the burial, the tearful days of sorting through clothes, books, memories. "I'll pray for you"...not just today and tomorrow, but at every Eucharist when we remember those living and those dead. It's a commitment to be part of a healing that will take a lifetime.

❧ TODAY: I will spend a few moments praying for my living friends who are dealing with the pain of death in their lives.

Give Me Space

I am not at ease, nor am I quiet;
  I have no rest; but trouble comes.—Job 3:26

A LITTLE SPACE, a few minutes to breathe, to regroup—not much to ask. But I'm surrounded on all sides by children in need.

"Mo-o-ommm!" echoes throughout the house, the word elongated to high-pitched multi-syllable pleas. I am needed...to break up fights, to pry open the puppy's mouth to retrieve a favorite doll, to check the health of a listless gerbil who "looks real funny, Mom," to sign a homework sheet, to correct the trial run of a math quiz, to laugh at the family's favorite comic strip, to untangle a knotted shoelace, to applaud achievements of my video game warriors, to supervise selections from the monthly book club, to give hugs for bruises, both physical and mental....I am mother; I am needed.

Always needing, my children are too young to know I am also in need...of a few minutes of not being needed. Forty-five minutes, not to lounge in front of the television, but to balance the checkbook. OK, I'll settle for thirty, to address a few Christmas cards and write uninterrupted, coherent sentences. Maybe I'm aiming too high: fifteen sounds great, enough time to draw the bath, fill it with bubbles, and reemerge refreshed. Not possible? How about five. Just five minutes in the bathroom alone—to sit, to quiet down, to muster up strength for the next onslaught.

"Just give me some space!" I sigh in desperation, and

my children back off, frightened by the tone of my request. They sense I've reached the end of my proverbial rope. So, newspaper in hand, I head off with instructions for the oldest to watch the youngest, close the door, and sit, savoring my time alone.

Then a thud and scratching interrupt my precious time that's already ticking away. A hairy head peeps through the door and a wet nose nudges my bare legs. My voice rises in a shrill scream of despair: "Just once, just today, can't somebody else let the dog out!"

લ TODAY: When I sense the approach of some quiet time, I'll leave even urgent tasks until later, and take a few minutes for myself so I can better meet my children's needs when the next round of requests begins.

Divorce

*For it has been reported to me by Chloe's people that
there are quarrels among you, my brothers and
sisters.—1 Corinthians 1:11*

I CAN TELL FROM THE INTENSITY of his voice and the
way he settles into the overstuffed chair, as if
expecting a long conversation, that the phone call
brings bad news. As our eyes meet, he covers the
mouthpiece and whispers the word I've already
anticipated: "Divorce."

The first in our families—why have I presumed we'd
be immune, when "breakup" has become almost a stage
in married life? But those cases, those cold statistics, have
in the past been about "them" not "us." Now it's us, our
relatives, an extension of our own family. Now the pain
radiating from the faces of neighbors or coworkers has
come closer; it's the pain in the voice of my brother-by-
marriage thousands of miles away penetrating phone
lines, reflected on my husband's face.

Distanced from that family, we have not really gotten
to know the wife or her children from a previous
marriage—a situation I've resented and regretted. But
now, knowing full well that no one person bears blame
for marital problems, I feel safe sympathizing with him;
she's more of a signature on a Christmas card than a
person who's suffering too.

They'll proceed quickly, with as little discord as
possible, to spare the children the ugliness that often
results from divorce. But no matter how good their

intentions, no one will be spared, especially the children. They're losing a father for a second time. Teens now, they'll strike a pose of nonchalance, as if immune to self-doubts and guilt. They'll alternately blame him and excuse her, and take it in stride, and move on with life...again. "Resilient"—that's the term they use about children of divorce, isn't it? How about the other words we choose to forget, like "vulnerable" and "scared"?

A trial separation early on, then family counseling— they had worked to salvage the family they were creating, to reignite the glow that had attracted them to one another. So I blame neither husband nor wife, hoping for happiness for both of them as they reshape their lives. But I grieve for the children whose fragile and constantly challenged self-concepts may make stability only an elusive word, a reality always just beyond their reach.

* TODAY: I will write or speak to friends going through separation or divorce to assure them of our prayers during this painful period in their lives.

Going It Alone

They heard how I was groaning,
with no one to comfort me.—Lamentations 1:21

I'VE HEARD THE STATISTICS, and I marvel at the spunk of all those single parents who daily raise their children alone. I am not one of them...except now, for a few days, when my husband's work calls him away from home.

It's not just the extra workload piled atop my already crammed day. It's more. It's the rhythm of our family that's been disturbed. Nothing drastic—but the timing's wrong. What was scored as allegro now moves like a child's first painful groping for the right notes.

Our lives together have been comfortable in a pattern no one's defined or scored, but we all know. One takes care of the dishes, while the other starts the baths; one helps with homework, while the other tackles the mounds of unsorted laundry. And each child has someone for nightly stories and back rubs before falling asleep.

We all feel the harmony temporarily disrupted. The children reflect back to me my frustration and inadequacy. "If Dad were home, he'd take us to the pool!" "Why do I have to carry out the trash?" No major uproars, only rumblings of discontent.

Before children, when he traveled for days, I felt strangely empty when he'd leave, back when family meant couple. Liberated, I took on the extra chores without flinching: What's so tough about dealing with mechanics or mowing the lawn? Then the house was too quiet, too empty without him.

Now the problem's not the solitude or silence—how I dream of that some nights. The house groans with the noise of slamming doors, barking dogs ("Will someone ple-ease let that dog out!"), and children's whines. Though the beat goes on, we're temporarily off key. But we can live a while longer with the dissonance, knowing that when the family's whole, we'll be back to making beautiful music, in sync and in harmony, once again.

❧ TODAY: I will set aside nonessential tasks so I can fill in for my children's missing parent, in hopes that we'll live in harmony until his return.

Road Trip Blues

For I am longing to see you....—Romans 1:11

M Y BAGS ARE PACKED, the children's schedules posted on the refrigerator, the day of departure has arrived. Already as I kiss them good-bye, I sense that this much-anticipated professional trip might have its drawbacks. Unused to travel, I have romanticized this weekend as the great getaway, the space for me to grow as career woman with an identity separate from motherhood.

And I do grow. I savor, at first, long-forgotten spans of uninterrupted time: an hour's reading on the plane, the chance to choose a TV channel without a protest, a hot meal with no little fingers picking at the plate because "yours always tastes better."

In the remote regions of consciousness, then gradually creeping forward until they rest comfortably near the nuggets of professional wisdom I'm absorbing, are thoughts of my children. I monitor my watch, noting between words of experts at the podium the times of my children's daily routines. Then, at a break, I head for souvenir shops, delighting in the choices of gifts for them.

Synchronizing my watch with clocks back home, I impatiently await the agreed-upon time to phone. I worry: Will they be as eager to talk as I am? "Hi, I miss you!" I gush as the phone passes from child to child, and greedily absorb the day's news. In the background, family noises of piano, television, sibling quarrels—noises I'd longed to escape, but now wish to embrace once more.

It was the right choice, shedding the mother role for a respite, to allow the professional me to thrive. What I've learned these few days will serve me well, bring me in step with my peers. More important, though, will be other knowledge, a confirmation of what I've suspected all along: that the "career me" and the "Mom me" are inextricably woven together. Who I am is not one or the other, but a harmonious blending of the two that don't merely coexist but that nurture one another to make me more fully me.

❧ TODAY: I will send home a postcard to my children telling them how much I miss them. When it arrives, I will reinforce in person the message of love I've sent.

A Joyful Noise

Make a joyful noise to God, all the earth.—Psalm 66:1

E VEN IN THE WOMB, so the parenting magazines all
say, children can hear and respond to music; my
imagination creates a picture of joyful
choreographed swimming and splashing in amniotic
waters.

Then, thrust out of that secure water into the glare of
light and the blare of noise, the newborn must grasp at
any remembrance of that life before life. For my children,
music becomes the new umbilical cord, tying us together.

Early on, I tapped into the rhythms of the generations,
adopting the stance and movement of my mother before
me, one she'd slip into as each new grandchild was
placed for the first time in her arms. It's the slow swaying
to some unheard melody that connects her to the baby
she holds. Nursing, changing diapers, pacing the house in
our nightly bout of colic, I turn to the old tunes I
remember from my childhood, ones my mother sang to
me or I learned at church. Somehow the music calms both

mother and child.

One family Christmas at the home of our childhood, two sisters and I try with little success to block out the noise and excitement so our babies will drop off to sleep. One of us begins to hum a tune each in our own time had sung with friends around the campfire: lively, at first, then with each verse, slowing down as all three children drop off to sleep. Where did it come from? Pondering the words now, I think it's a gospel song from a religion not my own, with unfamiliar words my children question as they grow old enough to understand. No matter, it does the job.

Even today, as they're old enough to soothe themselves to sleep listening to a radio by their beds or reading one more chapter of a book, they still ask for that special song—"all the verses, Mom"—and they rouse from sleep enough to remind me if I skip one.

Perhap someday they'll learn our ritual "soothing song"—not just the tune, but all twelve verses. Or they'll go to camp, seize a song and save it for children of their own. New songs or old, music is a constant that binds mother to child, connecting each generation.

❧ TODAY: I will sing to my child, or with my child, a special song, making it a song of praise to God for the gift of children and song.

Godchild

*See what love the Father has given us, that we should be
called children of God; and that is what we are.*
—1 John 3:1

"OH, GREAT," I GROAN to myself as we enter
church many Sunday mornings, "Why'd we
have to pick the Mass with baptisms!" Not one,
but four sets of parents with their crying babies lining up
behind the celebrant. These are my least favorite liturgies,
since multiple christenings add another ten minutes to an
already-long Sunday Mass, a significant time increase for
parents with three squirming children who keep asking,
"Is it almost over?"

But this Sunday is different: My husband and I are
among those proudly lining up in the back of church,
accompanying friends and their baby boy, our godchild.

This Sunday the mid-Mass baptisms that other days
seem to drag on forever hold my attention. The gentle
pastor crosses four foreheads with chrism, then trickles
water over each while pronouncing four Christian names.
As he lights four tapers from the paschal candle, I take to
heart his challenge to "keep this flame burning bright."

This baby boy, now a child of God, is called to walk by
Christ's light, and I am to be a guide on his journey. I am
flattered and a bit frightened at being chosen for this role.
Selecting godparents for our three children was not a task
my husband and I took lightly. Godparents were to be
models of Christian living, not just bestowers of special
gifts on birthdays, Christmases, graduations. By design

their lives will be entwined with our children's, as they share their spiritual gifts.

This sleeping infant cradled in his mother's arms is now bonded to me not by blood but by water. Now he hardly knows me, preferring his father's or mother's looks and touch and smell. But I won't let it remain that way for long. When I pronounce his name, John, I will be reminded of another John, the chronicler of light and love, the narrator of the story of his forerunner, John the baptizer. I will remember these words by and about my godchild's namesakes: "Whoever loves his brothers and sisters lives in the light" and "Little children, let us love, not in word or speech, but in truth and action" and "He himself was not the light, but he came to testify to the light."

As this child of God grows and wraps himself around my heart, he will remind me of what I should be not only for him but for my own children: not the light, but a bearer of the Light, the Word made flesh that I can make more visible in a sometimes-darkened world.

☙ TODAY: I will send a message of gratitude to the parents of my godchild for entrusting me with the special role of godmother.

High-Energy Zone

A S THE ALARM BLURTS its early-morning reveille,
I roll out of bed with less energy and more
aches than usual. No wake-up exercises for this
body today, I groan, wondering why my calves and
thighs are throbbing. Then I remember: Yesterday, in a
frolicsome mood, I had accepted my children's invitation
to "come up and play with us, Mom. Grownups are
allowed up here."

Why not? I'd asked myself. Other moms are
scrambling up ladders and zipping down slides with
their children. What's stopping me?

The morning after the question is: What should have
stopped me? For starters, my age. Looking back on the
scene, I recall wondering whether those other women
were babysitters or big sisters, as young as they looked.
Another good-sense deterrent: my out-of-condition body.
The others' athletic sweatsuits and stretch outfits should
have clued me in that those adults probably spend more
waking hours in a week than I do in a year power-
walking or measuring their heartbeats during aerobic
exercise class.

So, for reasons of physical health, I should have
declined my children's invitation. But I didn't. Just the
glint of surprise in their eyes when I accepted told me this
would be an event not soon forgotten, one that would be
embellished and passed on during tall tale times at family
gatherings. Their aging mom was more of a sport than

they had imagined.

"Slow down!" I pleaded, as they scampered up steep, child-size steps to the tunnel slide. "Your turn!" they screamed in delight at the bottom of a tunnel from which I prayed I'd eventually emerge if my claustrophobia didn't get the better of me. "Look down," they teased, together leaning over the edge of the highest platform, aware that fear of heights was carried in a gene that had skipped their generation. Then the best: legs wrapped around one another, we sailed together down a roller slide that bumped our bottoms as the force of my body behind theirs accelerated us beyond their wildest imaginings. Hitting the bottom, luckily cushioned for such falls, we emerged giggling from a tangled heap.

The giggles, the eyes opened in disbelief that their mother would be so foolish, so daring, to match her aging body with ones so vigorous, the protests when "enough is enough and it's dinnertime" ended the adventure. These memories, long etched in my mind, are worth all the aches of the morning after.

❧ TODAY: Instead of sitting on the sidelines as a spectator, I will enter into physical play with my children (within the limits of reason, of course).

Peals of Laughter

*And all the people went up following him, playing on
pipes and rejoicing with great joy, so that the earth
quaked at their noise.—1 Kings 1:40*

"C'MON, MOM, JUST THIS ONCE. We'll even ride at
the same time. It's only a quarter." Lately,
they'd given up asking, so used were they to my
firm refusal—they were too big to ride the horse outside
the grocery store, the horse that had swallowed up
quarter after quarter when they were toddlers, the horse
whose music squeaked and skipped on a wornout tape.

But today, I relent, reminding them not to pester me
again. I should have known this would be no simple
get-on-then-get-off adventure. Two children too big to
ride solo squirm for proper positioning so neither will
fall. "Just put the quarter in!" I yell, feigning public
nonchalance about the frozen food dangerously near
room temperature. Not yet, they say, the horse needs a
name and a few strokes on its painted mane.

Finally, scrunched together on a saddle built for
toddler-sized bottoms, they lean over to drop the quarter
in the slot. Music reverberating down the corridor, the
horse jolts into action, accompanied by squeals of delight
as the two riders deliberately slip precariously near the
tail or down the saddle. Staid shoppers push by without
noticing, while others smile in delight.

It is funny, I admit to myself, forgetting the ice cream
and the frozen peas turning to mush in my cart. Riding
the horse at age six and nine is a greater adventure than

years ago. The incongruity is not lost on them. Too old to ride authentically, yet still small enough to fit, they revel in memories of excitement. Heads bounce in exaggerated imitation of past rides when they really were too little and really were frightened that they might fall off. Now, in control, they subdue the horse with peals of laughter that rock their bodies until their sides hurt.

The music over, they take leave of the well-worn horse with dramatic flourishes and excessive kisses. Giddy, refreshed, they seem temporarily purged of the burdens of modern life through a few minutes of silliness. Such a bargain for only twenty-five cents.

ᏺ TODAY: When my children get silly, I will allow them the joy of the experience, trying not to squelch their fun with reminders of deadlines and dangers.

Liturgy the Joyful Way

Clap your hands, all you peoples;
shout to God with loud songs of joy.—*Psalm 47:1*

A BREAK FOR A WEAK AND WEEK-WEARY SPIRIT—
that's why I savor joyful liturgies. Here people
gather, strangers for just a while, because they
want to gather; here people know how to celebrate and be
exuberant.

Too often I enter my parish church, a sacred space,
with nothing sacred on my mind. I plunk myself and my
children into a pew out of guilt, out of social pressure, out
of habit. I don't really choose to be there. I'm not focused,
I'm out of tune with my inner feelings. Those around me
are strangers...and I want them to remain that way.

But on special occasions my needs and the celebration
converge. Something inside me resonates with the joy of
the moment. These celebrations are Celebrations. The
readings reflect my journeylings or hint at my future.
When I listen to the homilist's thoughts on Scripture,
those thoughts echo mine—my frustrations, my joys, my
humanness in search of the divine.

The rituals, so often antiquated or stale, tap something
primal, something sacred in my depths. I want to dance
with the dancer swirling banners through the church. The
blessed water rolls off my forehead as a soulmate, no
longer "that stranger next to me," dips into the font to
trace a cross of blessing on me. My tears mingle with
water as the blessings multiply around me.

We need worship, we need symbol. We are a

ritual-starved people hardly satiated by Super Bowl halftimes and seventh-inning stretches. Sometimes it's only through the concrete, the physical, earthly elements like fire and water that we can express our deepest longings. We are a people in need of songs belted out with gusto to replace the vapid, half-hearted mumblings of most Sunday mornings.

We tolerate dead, obligatory liturgies imposed on our week—sadly the norm rather than the exception. But we come to life, we're awakened, by ceremonies that link us through symbol and song with God and with one another.

&. TODAY: I resolve that the next liturgical celebration I attend—a Sunday Mass, a funeral, a wedding, a baptism— I will participate fully to help enrich the worship of those around me.

Family Gatherings

How very good and pleasant it is
when kindred live together in unity!—Psalm 133:1

OUR GATHERINGS ARE PERIODIC and predictable—
yearly like summer's long-awaited lightning
bugs, or less frequent like the cyclic cicadas—
reminding me of roots and connections.

From the east, a sister and her family, the older
children hovering around their newborn sibling to the
delight of grandparents and the frustration of cousins
who want a chance to walk and rock her.

From my native city, aunts and uncles not seen in
years, reminding me of my own childhood with tales to
delight my children. "When your mom was little..." "Do
you remember the time when...?" My children's eyes
light up as they tuck away in their memories one of my
misadventures or blunders; they'll retrieve it as
ammunition when the time is right.

And my cousins with their own children—could we
have all grown so old so quickly? I'm transported back
thirty years as their children, modern only in dress and
slang, greet me with smiles or mannerisms that mimic
their parents' decades earlier.

Conversations, at first halting and fragmented by
introductions of late arrivals, deepen as groups and pairs
splinter off to resume relationships interrupted a year
earlier. With halting, unspoken permission, we move
beyond baseball rivalries and children's achievements to
matters of depth: the economic crunch of a job layoff, the

challenge of teenagers, the anxiety of watching a father deteriorate with Parkinson's Disease.

Cameras are as plentiful as coolers and baseball mitts. We line up, welcoming one or two more wiggly babies, hoping they'll face forward at the pop of a dozen flashes. Months later, as I sort through pictures still unlabeled despite my good intentions, I compare this reunion with the last. I note the unfailing pattern of life and death that's ritualized in these gatherings: new children and spouses temper the sadness of recently-dead aunts, uncles, grandparents. Family reunions—periodic reminders that, like all of God's creatures, we're linked with one another in the cycle of life.

ᘒ TODAY: I will take time to write a brief note to some relative who was a significant part of my youth, just to keep in touch between family gatherings.

Savoring That Perfect Evening

*Better is a dinner of vegetables where love is
than a fatted ox and hatred with it.—Proverbs 15:17*

SOMETIMES IT JUST all falls together, that perfect
family meal. Not when you plan on it—those
evenings with the wedding china and the linen
tablecloth and the gourmet meal (we *will* learn some
manners)—but more often the leftover or the carryout-
pizza kind of thrown-together dinner.

But it clicks: the children in play clothes sweaty from
an afternoon on swings or bikes or in trees, parents
letting down after a day of work, bracing for the jostling
and the whining that the end of the day often brings. But
tonight it brings only smiles, good appetites and a
"Please" with the "pass the salt."

This is how families live in books, on television, in our
pre-children dreams. But not every day, not usually. So
we tiptoe through the beginnings of the meal—the
prayer, the choice of beverage, the first conversations of
"How was your day?" Then we relax, knowing this is
somehow different, a serendipitous evening. Time to
scrap our plans of finishing that project (it's already late),
cleaning up the day's dishes and getting the children to
bed on time.

Weeks from now, when we're back to the routine,
when the stresses of the day catch up with us at dinner
time, when mealtimes resemble the eye of the hurricane
more than islands in the sun, let me remember this night
and savor it, as an unexpected gift from a God who takes

seriously a mother's too familiar pathetic cry, "Give me a break!"

❧ TODAY: I will take dinner time in stride. I'll accept whatever it brings—pandemonium or peace. I won't let the "little things" turn the meal into armed warfare.

Life's Bounty

What shall I return to the LORD for all his bounty to me?—Psalm 116:12

THE SCENE, WITH VARIATIONS LINKED to age differences, occurs daily in supermarkets and shopping malls everywhere. A cereal, a toy, a pair of trendy shoes inspire "need" in children who feel deprived compared with their peers.

"You want it, but you don't really need it," I and countless other mothers preach in voices subdued yet firm. "Look how much you have, more than you could ever need."

"More than you could ever need"—the words echo as a judgment against me when I find myself striving for more. Not as blatant as my children's fabricated needs, but just as much a product of greed: a suit I can function professionally without, an upscale fountain pen, lunch at an "in" restaurant. Like my children, I must learn to appreciate the blessings enriching my life, especially the human ones I often take for granted.

To begin with, my children. Sure, if they weren't a part of my life, I'd have more money for the suits, the pens, the dinners, but in my children is a richness beyond measure. My daily bounty is more than bread and drink; I am nourished by their affection, their dependence, their innocence, their candor. When I'm down, they sense it and add an extra hug before bedtime. When I think the world has become a dark, hardened place in which to live, they redeem me by a prophetic insight about human nature or a spontaneous gesture of generosity to someone in real need.

My bounty reaches beyond them to those who love them: relatives who send birthday cards, specially chosen to delight a child—a card for the receiver rather than the sender; friends who offer to babysit at just the moment when I think I've forgotten how to talk to my husband as husband rather than as father of our children; coworkers who adapt work schedules to accommodate my emergency trip to school for an ill child.

Too often I forget to remind myself of the same lessons my parents shared with me. Appreciating the fullness of God's bounty—that's a goal that will take a lifetime to achieve.

ۥ TODAY: As I move through stores I will remind myself to buy out of need, not just frivolous desires.

Birthday Joys

*I do not remember to have ever met a slave who could
tell of his birthday. They seldom come nearer to it than
planting-time, harvest-time, cherry-time, spring-time,
or fall-time. A want of information concerning my own
was a source of unhappiness to me even during
childhood.*—Frederick Douglass, Narrative of the Life
of an American Slave

NO BIRTHDAYS—what a deprivation for anyone,
especially for a child.

Christmas often brings more gifts than
birthdays, Valentine's Day more cards, Easter and
Halloween more sweets, but birthdays win hands-down
for a day of basking in the spotlight.

First birthdays hold a special place in a family's
memory, often recorded on film or videotape as the
milestones they are. Usually, these days aren't as much
fun for the birthday child as for parents and siblings, who
watch expectantly for their baby's foray into piles of
wrapped gifts (who cares what's inside, let's eat the
paper and ribbon), for wide eyes as the candle flames
atop the cake, for delight at eyes focused on him as he
squishes baby fingers into inch-high frosting.

First birthdays behind them, children quickly catch
on: This is their day, but one too slow in getting here.
"How long till my birthday?" becomes the refrain months
before the special day. With each sibling's or friend's
party, the anticipation builds for this day of days.

It's not just the cake and the gifts, though without

them birthdays surely would be less festive. For the very young, birthdays mark concrete steps out of childhood toward the age of privilege, always a few years out of their reach.

"How old are you?" elicits specifics beyond whole numbers—"five" quickly becomes "five and a half," then "almost six." Guessing a child's age is risky business for adults used to complimenting friends by guessing too low; for kids the rule is, err high if you're going to err.

Birthdays mean privileges, being prince or princess for the day. "I'll get it for you, because it's your birthday." "You can ride my bike, just today, because it's your birthday." "Why do we have to have this for dinner?" "Because she chose it...and it's her birthday."

Birthdays mean marking off the days on calendars or pulling off the loops of paper chains, then looking for telltale signs of progress: "When do you think I'll start getting birthday cards?"—the first hard evidence that it won't be much longer now. And the birthday eve: "I can't get to sleep, tomorrow's my birthday." That morning, will we trick her into thinking we've forgotten what day it is, or will we wake her early for a birthday hug?

By day's end, after birthday "paddling," choruses of "Happy Birthday," phone calls from aunts, uncles and grandparents, and cake for dessert and bedtime snack, the birthday child begins to resist reality, putting off bedtime to stretch this event out forever. It's a bittersweet time of day: still her own precious hours, but a signal that the next day on the throne (unless you're lucky enough to live in a family that celebrates half-birthdays or unbirthdays) is an unfathomable 365 days away. So to sleep now...and let the countdown begin!

❧ TODAY: I will mark my child's birthday not only with gifts but with an extra walk or talk or a personal message on a birthday card.

Easter Visions

But the angel said to the women, "Do not be afraid;
I know that you are looking for Jesus who was crucified.
He is not here; for he has been raised, as he said."
—*Matthew 28:5-6*

EASTER A FEW HUNDRED MILES FROM HOME, but it may as well be continents away for all the strangeness in the celebration. For a holiday built on tradition, we can find little to connect us to our family's past.

First, the Easter bunny had arrived early, the day before Easter, so that the ritual of finding baskets and eggs could be preserved. For all their delight ("How did he know we wouldn't be here tomorrow?"), the children had sensed the difference. Unprepared to find the bunny's note about hidden treasures, they had missed out on preliminary rituals—the night-before struggle to get to sleep as visions of chocolate bunnies danced in their heads, the morning countdown as they waited for the parent-appointed time to race down the steps and let the hunt begin. This year's surrogate Easter at home on Holy Saturday had fallen flat.

Part II—Easter morning. Mass at an out-of-town church. Besides being unknown to us, the families crowding into pews look foreign, Americans hailing from lands unfamiliar to us; names in the parish bulletin twist our tongues as we try to pronounce them. So what if we're not celebrating with friends, I remind myself, we are all the Body of Christ. The Mass, crammed with high-church rituals executed in elaborate detail, does little to awaken in me the joy of the resurrection, but as an adult, I am able to compensate by remembering Easters past and vowing never to leave home again on important liturgical feasts.

The children, less philosophical, periodically remind me how unmoved they are by the "celebration." Confronted by a six-foot-high wall of Easter bonnets and suits blocking any view of the action on the altar or the lectern, one whispers, "I feel like I'm watching Mass on TV." "How many more songs?" complains another, ten minutes into the Mass. "Too many to count," I reply, sighing in sympathy and knowing it is useless to point out similarities with our home parish since the differences are so prominent, beginning with the pre-Mass recitation of the rosary right through bells at the Consecration. At the Lord's Prayer, we join hands as is our custom at our parish. "No one else is holding hands," my eight-year-old observes, trying to let loose of my grip. I cling tightly, as much to the tradition as to her hand.

We had come looking for the risen Jesus. He was there, the Scriptures assured me. Like the women confounded by an empty tomb, I wasn't sure what I'd experienced that morning. I left still searching for meaning, only through an act of faith acknowledging that I'd met the Christ in the breaking of the bread and the sharing of prayer with unfamiliar people on an Easter morning far away from home.

&❧ TODAY: I will celebrate Easter fully—despite the crowded church, despite flaws in the liturgy, trying to remember the essence of the resurrection event rather than focusing on externals.

Reborn in Spring

What is all this juice and all this joy?
A strain of the earth's sweet being in the beginning
In Eden garden.—Gerard Manley Hopkins, "Spring"

FINALLY. AFTER MONTHS of dusky daytimes, grass brown from winter dormancy, blackened snow piled high in parking lots. Finally, signs of spring, following a week of blizzards and record snowfalls in neighboring states. We've been lucky—a few inches of snow and a hazardous night of driving; it's the front-page pictures and tales from harried relatives and friends that remind us of winter's grip.

So spring's sudden entry surprises us all. Bud casings litter the sidewalk; oak leaves newly fallen from nearby trees crunch underfoot, then cling to our wet shoes each time we come indoors. A lone wasp buzzes around the eaves of the house.

With spring's return come annual irritations: gym shoes soggy from play in the rain-soaked yard, muddy paw prints recording the dog's trail through the house, drawers and closets bulging from two sets of clothes to meet the demands of unpredictable temperatures.

But even I can forgive the messes and the extra work when I measure them against the vigor spring has infused in our lives. My children hurry through meals to squeeze a few more minutes of play from each lengthening day. Television and video games go untouched for days—how can machines indoors compete with Frisbees and softball and bikes and rollerskates? Off go the sweats and on go the shorts, even on days too cold for summer wear—no one can wait to cast aside the remnants of winter.

Crocuses and daffodils inch up, then bloom, as if recorded through time-lapsed photography. Scents of flowers waft into the house through open windows. There's a sweetness and a newness in the air.

Soon we will grow used to it. Spring and its joys will become routine. We'll forget to note the fat robin pecking at the grass and the forsythia lining the park entrance, the sun baking the closed-up car. But now we bask in spring's gifts, grateful for this yearly participation in God's creative power, the closest we'll ever know of earlier Edens.

🙜 TODAY: I will take some time to be with my children outdoors to celebrate the newness of the season: rake leftover leaves from flower beds, walk the dog, play in the park.

Mother's Day

Her children rise up and call her happy;
her husband too, and he praises her:
"Many women have done excellently,
but you surpass them all."—Proverbs 31:28-29

IT'S ANOTHER HECTIC SUNDAY MORNING as we prod children from bed for 9:30 Mass, but in the midst of the chaos, we pause: They can wait no longer to share the Mother's Day gifts that have been hidden all week. How I look forward to Mother's Day, one day a year to overdose on sentimental expressions of affection.

My husband's comes first in a small box, hummingbird earrings, and a card too emotional to read aloud, "To My Wife, the Most Beautiful Part of My Life." I'll savor it later in leisure.

"I'm first."

"No, me. You were first last time."

The winner of the quarrel displays for my

appreciation a potted plant bought at school ("I need two dollars for school. It's a surprise," she'd begged the week before). From another, a window-sill jar filled with flowers, water and "snow," presented with tears: "It's leaking. The glue was too old. I'm gonna throw it away."

Then come the cards—homemade, each child's personality stamped so clearly that signatures seem superfluous. From my youngest, a six-pager shaped like a flower pot, "The Best Mom in the World, by Annie," in which she expresses her gratitude and delineates my roles in the home: "Thank you mom for washing my clothes, for feeding the dog, for helping me with my homework, for going grocery shopping with me, for reading me a story at night." A fully illustrated treasure, documenting my contributions to the family (despite constant complaints from children: "How come I have to do all the work around here?").

From my quieter, middle child, a fluorescent orange card decorated with delicate flowers, each petal cut then pasted. Inside, a simple message in pictorial symbols: "Eye heart u! From Liz" (her last name hastily erased— she must have forgotten this was not a typical class assignment).

From my oldest, a pre-teen, an age-appropriate message, sincere but far from gushy: "I love you so much. You're the greatest mother. Thanks for putting up with me."

Not the gauzy pastel picture of Mother's Day portrayed on posters in card stores, this Mother's Day is a microcosm of real family life, with all its vying for attention, disappointment and tears, and understated expressions of love.

Yet, in her own way, each child has paid tribute to me as mother. Their cards, in a diversity that mirrors each one's creativity, tell me that as their mother, I am deserving of a special love, I reflect as I hurry them off to finish dressing and brush teeth so we won't be late for church. Then I notice that in the excitement of unwrapping and reading, I've missed a message on one of the cards.

A monkey? What's a monkey doing on a Mother's Day card? I'm sure it's a sweet rhyme from one of my own little monkeys, some emotional tribute to set the tone for my day.

Well, not quite: "I love you. I love you. But don't get excited. I love monkeys too."

So much for sentimentality!

❧ TODAY: I will sit back and cherish this Mother's Day, with all its confusion, conflict and affection.

Father's Day: To My Husband

Wife, for all you know, you might save your husband.
Husband, for all you know, you might save your
wife.—1 Corinthians 7:16

THE GIFTS ARE NEVER THE HARD PART; you're a shopper's dream, so transparent in the hints you drop weeks before the actual day—"just in case you want a few ideas for Father's Day...."

But the card presents another problem, aisles and aisles of them to choose from and never just the right one. Yours has to be perfect, destined as it is to join the stack bulging from your second dresser drawer, the one weighted down by memories of our life together.

The children, entertaining themselves long after they choose their card, have little patience with my pursuit of perfection: too sentimental or too "masculine" (you don't hunt and you don't smoke a pipe), too serious or too corny, too prosaic or too poetic, too secular or too religious.

I guess I'll have to write one myself.

"Happy Father's Day to the man I love." Nah, too typical and predictable.

"Honey, I love you more than you could ever know"—not true. You know as well as I the depth of my love...and once in a while have to remind me to say it aloud.

Once I came close to saying it just right, the weekend of your renewal experience at the parish. That letter is probably somewhere in a pile preserved with every other card and note from the past seventeen years, but it's easier to search my heart than your cluttered drawer.

I love you.

I love you as father to our children: at their birth, consoling and cheering and crying with me over the miracles we had created in our love for one another; in their growth—sometimes prodding, sometimes pampering, often standing back with a quiet smile of joy or recognition at how much of both of us you see in them; in their sorrow, hurting with them and hiding your anger (from all but me) that their lives have been touched by pain; in their moving outward, letting them go better than I can ever do—to take longer bike rides, climb higher trees, test unknown waters.

But since there's more to you than just your father side, I'll say today how I love you just for who you are: complex yet simple; outwardly gruff but inside a pushover to those who know your weak spot, that mushy core where you nurture and cherish those blessed enough to be loved by you; cynical at the hardness of the world, but open enough to give to and forgive the pure of heart.

And I love you for who you are to me—a gentle lover, a firm supporter, my safety valve in times of stress, my level when my life shifts out of balance.

"Clone him," my friends say in disbelief as I talk with pride of your exploits as "family man." But I decline. You alone aren't what makes you such a prize; it's that happy blending of you with me.

On this Father's Day I wish you love and a good meal (maybe I'll cook it and give you the day off) and a few hours of harmony among our children, and many more Father's Days together.

"Here's lookin' at you."

❦ TODAY: In my prayer at Mass, I will thank God for the blessing my husband has been in my life, to me and to our children.

Autumn Arrives

Margaret are you grieving
Over Goldengrove unleaving?
—Gerard Manly Hopkins, "Spring and Fall"

SOME YEAR I'LL LEARN to read the hints from nature so I won't be shocked by the "sudden" change in season: the spiders moving indoors for warmth, the v's of ducks overhead as we head to the car from the football stadium, the precocious tree that already stands bereft of leaves as color begins to touch its neighbors.

Autumn is here, and I'm not yet prepared...for its chores and its gifts. Finally I am forced, by children with chilled legs, to sort the summer shorts and T-shirts from drawers bulging with hot- and cold-weather gear to accommodate the wishy-washy weather of September. Porch furniture, still occasionally useful, stands draped in yellow maple leaves; it's time to cart those chairs indoors.

Gutters, overflowing with water from the week's rain, spew out leaves clogging the drainage path.

For the moment, I ignore autumn's chores in favor of its annual wonders. The smell of neighborhood fireplaces drifts through the evening air, as I gather wood to light our family's fire. On my daily journey to work, even the irritation of slow-moving traffic diminishes as I absorb the ever-changing colors of the hillsides. At backyard bird feeders, regular visitors pause to acknowledge the presence of a bird of prey passing through—a hawk, obviously sidetracked in the suburbs, sits on the branch above the feeders to size up the neighborhood, then return to the wilds.

And best of all, the leaves. They await us as either chore or challenge, piling up to bury tree roots and sidewalks. Rakes in hand, we dive into the task, then into the pile, scattering our afternoon's efforts. But it's worth repeating the job. After all, autumn disappears as quickly as the raked leaves, once splendid on trees, now crumbling beneath the weight of our bodies. Soon we'll be left with only memories, until autumn reappears to thrill and surprise us next year.

æ TODAY: Instead of complaining about autumn chores, I will celebrate it, with a family "let's look at the leaves" ride or a leaf-raking party.

The Warmth of Fire

Praise to Thee, my Lord, for Brother Fire,
By whom Thou lightest the night;...
—Francis of Assisi, "Canticle of the Creatures"

ALL SUMMER THE WOOD PILE has stood neglected.
The sparse stack has needed no attention, so
I've not complained of its other uses: a fort for
protection against neighborhood invaders, a home for
"pioneer" babies, a shortcut through the yard for
squirrels (and kids). But September is here, with its
on-again, off-again chilling mornings, and my thoughts
turn to autumn. Time to replenish the wood.

We trek through the nearby park for stray pieces of
tinder and kindling that belong to no one but the earth.
Small hands reach down for pieces to add to the
now-growing bundle. "Is this too green, Mom?" "Is this
one OK?" The stick-gathering preliminaries over, we
await delivery of the "real" wood—a truckload dumped
in our yard and hauled in wagonloads to be stacked
end-to-end in the back, untouched until just the right day
for the first fire of the season.

It comes. Already that morning we know this will be
the perfect night. The morning air is so cold that we blow
frosty breath into the air. The African violet plants have
to be rescued from the front porch to protect late-
blooming flowers. There's a crisp feeling to the day that
we're sure won't disappear by evening.

As dusk approaches we haul the most perfect pieces to
the hearth: the brittle twigs that snap with the smallest

twist, the crusty branches we'll break for starter logs, some leftovers seasoned all summer on the diminished pile. The wind picks up, whistling down the chimney as we flip open the flue.

One match does the trick. We cuddle on couches, wrapped in blankets dug from summer storage. Our eyes mirror one another's joy as flames lick the fireplace bricks and spread through the seasoned wood. We savor the past months' memories as we bid good-bye to the heat of summer outdoors and embrace the warmth and the light of the fire within.

❧ TODAY: We'll spend time together as a family, enjoying the warmth of our home and each other.

Thanksgiving Day

The earth has yielded its increase;
God, our God, has blessed us.—Psalm 67:6

T HE TURKEY, WHAT'S LEFT OF IT, has been tucked on the bottom shelf of the fridge still on the china platter, to be nibbled on tomorrow. The dining room table, a few hours earlier blanketed with food, now looks barren, the crumbs and cranberry stains the sole witnesses to the feast we've shared. The children, exhausted from too much food and too much romping, sleep upstairs, while I sit before the dying fire to take stock of blessings of this day:

For a family to spend Thanksgiving with—for nurturing parents, saintly aunts, loving siblings;

For potatoes peeled around the kitchen table, for three generations of hands and hearts joined in that simple and symbolic task;

For the spirit of sharing that makes a feast out of one sister's beans, another's homegrown potatoes, a mother's pumpkin pies;

For the "increase" the earth has yielded so that our Thanksgiving table overflows with food;

For prayer offered before the meal as we join hands to thank God for a year filled with blessings;

For safe journeys, from long distances and short, that bring us here and take us back again;

For stories embellished between grandfather and grandchild, the two bonding over travels and tigers and first-grade classmates;

For the warmth of a family who opens their day to a family-less friend, welcoming him without reservations or questions;

For toddlers climbing everywhere, rescued over and over again from near disaster by vigilant parents and aunts—without a break in the conversation;

For all our children, who articulate their thanks in their freely given hugs and their sleepy kisses as they're carried to cars for late-night trips home;

For these and all your blessings throughout the year, I thank you, Lord.

🕭 TODAY: As we bless our Thanksgiving meal that we share, I will offer a special prayer of gratitude for the riches God has brought into my life.

Holiday Horrors

*Deck the halls with boughs of holly, Fa-la-la-la-la,
la-la-la-la. 'Tis the season to be jolly, Fa-la-la-la-la,
la-la-la-la.*—Traditional Christmas carol

HOLIDAYS. FOR MOTHERS, they're certainly not holydays. More like horrordays. Christmas, Easter, Valentine's Day—all were meant to remind us of another life, a higher good, to bring us back to the source, our Beginning and our End.

More often, though, they plunge us more deeply into the murkiness of this world to remind us of our need for salvation. Holidays are no breaks for moms. A time to relax? Never. In our "free" time, we're shopping, cleaning, organizing, budgeting, breaking up fights, cooking, then cleaning up from the ravages of this "break."

More challenging, though, is the children's free time. Used to the structure of their daily routine, they often wallow aimlessly in a formless holi-daze. "I'm bored, what can I do?" How about reading? Or writing thank-you notes, or riding your bike? "Naw, I've done all that. I mean something fun." And as every mother who has "celebrated" a holiday and lived to tell her tale can attest, in the midst of formlessness, a basic law of physics rules all: "For every action there's an equal and opposite reaction." Mom acts ("If you're bored, try cleaning your room") and child reacts ("If you don't like it, close the door and don't look at it"); sibling acts ("That outfit looks stupid") and another sibling reacts ("Mom, tell her to get out of my room!").

Holidays—days of goodwill, family harmony, remembrance of the Savior's birth or death or resurrection to bring us all new life, photo-album moments to look back on with nostalgia in years to come. These romanticized notions do us no good. We set our sights too high, imagining holidays as feel-good days that offer respite from our humdrum lives. I say, back to the humdrum. I'll revel in the routine, setting the alarm early for the first day back after my "break," so I can cherish every moment of my mundane existence. Holidays— they're OK to visit, but I wouldn't want to live there.

❧ TODAY: I will reflect on the spiritual significance of the holiday we're celebrating and try to plan one small activity for my children that reflects the true meaning of the occasion.

A New Year

To be free, to be able to stand up
  and leave everything behind—
without looking back. To say Yes.
—*Dag Hammarskjöld*, Markings

N
EW YEAR'S EVE—a time to step back and take
stock of the old year and plan for the new.
Difficult to do, without a few mea culpas,
without some trepidation.

There have been better years. But would they have
been better for me at this time in my life? No use
second-guessing: This is the year that was.

It held more than its share of pain: illnesses, too often
and too severe; friendships strained from lack of
nurturing; cutbacks in family income; relatives out of
work; cars and appliances refusing to hang on just one
more year.

Those aspects were out of my control, but other
disappointing turns I must take responsibility for. Too
quickly the year sped by without enough self-
transformation: not enough exercise—physical or
spiritual; not enough patience; not enough quality time
with my family; not enough phone calls to friends and
relatives; not enough play in my life.

But enough self-flagellation. The clock is ticking away
the hours until midnight. Less than half a day left of the
old year, hardly worth investing time to salvage its
remains. The new year awaits creation.

Long ago I gave up the ritual of New Year's

Resolutions. Hastily scribbled on a piece of paper January 1, they were often lost or broken by mid-month. "I'll exercise more." "I'll be more generous, more patient." "I'll write more often." Some failure aids humility, but defeat year after year wears me down.

This year my resolution will be more abstract and general—the easiest and the hardest type to keep. I will approach the future with open arms. It's a stance of acceptance, but not passivity. I cannot control the future, but I can help shape it. "YES!"—so easy to write, so difficult to live. What this word means, what it will bring into my life, I can't predict. Like Dag Hammarskjöld, I will pray, "For all that has been thanks; for all that will be yes."

❧ TODAY: I will formalize my resolution of saying "yes" to the future by reading the "annunciation" passage in Scripture (Luke 1:26-38).

Acknowledgments

Scripture quotations are from the *New Revised Standard Version of the Bible*, copyright ©1989 by the Division of Christian Education of the National Council of the Churches of Christ in the USA. Used by permission. All rights reserved.

The excerpt from *Sponsorship* by the Sisters of Charity is used with the permission of the Sisters of Charity of Cincinnati Communications Office, Mount St. Joseph, Ohio, 45051.

The excerpt from "There is no frigate like a book" by Emily Dickinson reprinted by permission of the publishers and the Trustees of Amherst College from *The Poems of Emily Dickinson*, Thomas H. Johnson, ed., Cambridge, Mass.: The Belknap Press of Harvard University Press, copyright ©1951, 1955, 1979, 1983 by the President and Fellows of Harvard College.

The excerpt from *St. Francis of Assisi: Omnibus of Sources*, edited by Marion A. Habig, copyright ©1973 by Franciscan Herald Press, is reprinted with permission of Franciscan Press.

The excerpt from "The Goodnight" from *Collected Poems* by Louis Simpson, copyright ©1988 by Paragon House Publishers, is reprinted with permission of Paragon House Publishers.

Excerpts from *Markings* by Dag Hammarskjöld, trans., L. Sjoberg, W.H. Auden. Translation copyright ©1964 by Alfred A. Knopf, Inc., and Faber and Faber Ltd. Reprinted by permission of Alfred A. Knopf, Inc.

The excerpt from "The First Shoe" by Marie Mhac an tSaoi, translated from the Gaelic by Brendan O'Hehir, is taken from *The Other Voice*, edited by Joanna Bankier, copyright ©1976 by W.W. Norton & Co., Inc.

The excerpt from "The Man" by Nina Cassian is taken from *The Other Voice*, edited by Joanna Bankier, copyright ©1976 by W.W. Norton & Co., Inc., and was originally published by Peter Owen Ltd., London, England.

The excerpt from "Random Thoughts on the Love of God" by Simone Weil is taken from *The Other Voice*, edited by Joanna Bankier, copyright ©1976 by W.W. Norton & Co., Inc., and was originally published by Editions Gallimard, 5, rue Sebastien-Bottin, F-75007 Paris, France.

The excerpt from "Stay by Me" by Erich Sylvester copyright ©1972 by North American Liturgy Resources, Phoenix, Arizona.

The excerpt from "The Rime of the Ancient Mariner" by Samuel Taylor Coleridge is taken from *The Poems of Samuel Taylor Coleridge*, originally published by Oxford University Press, London.

The excerpts from "Spring" and "Spring and Fall" by Gerard Manley Hopkins were originally published by Oxford University Press.

The excerpt from "On His Blindness" by John Milton is taken from *Sound and Sense: An Introduction to Poetry*, edited by Laurence Perrine, published by Harcourt Brace and World, Inc.

The excerpt from "Narrative of the Life of Frederick Douglass, an American Slave" is taken from *The Heath Anthology of American Literature*, vol. I, published by D.C. Heath and Co., Lexington, Mass.